PIERCING
TIME
&
SPACE

PIERCING TIME & SPACE

WHERE SCIENCE AND SPIRIT MEET

Traci L. Slatton

ASSOCIATION FOR
RESEARCH AND
ENLIGHTENMENT

A.R.E. Press • Virginia Beach • Virginia

A.R.E. Press
215 67th Street
Virginia Beach, VA 23451-2061

Library of Congress Cataloguing-in-Publication Data
Slatton, Traci L.
Piercing time & space / by Traci L. Slatton
    p.   cm.
ISBN 0-87604-507-7 (trade paperback)
1. Parapsychology. 2. Cayce, Edgar, 1877-1945. 3. Occult sciences. I. Title: Piercing time and space. II. Title
BF1031.S56 2005
133.8—dc22

2005023989

Cover design by Richard Boyle

For Naomi, Jessica, Madeleine, and Sabin.

Contents

Acknowledgments .... *ix*

Introduction .... *xi*

Chapter One 1

Chapter Two 15

Chapter Three 31

Chapter Four 47

Chapter Five 67

Chapter Six 81

Chapter Seven 99

Notes *109*

Bibliography *115*

Acknowledgments

I would like to thank the inestimable Dr. Henry Grayson, whose remark about the oneness of the unified fields, Akashic Records, and morphic fields inspired the idea for this book. I would also like to thank Mr. Ken Skidmore for championing my writing and being intrigued by these ideas. Martha Millard, agent extraordinaire, also deserves many kudos. My husband Sabin Howard read every page and scribbled comments both funny and insightful, for which I am profoundly grateful. My daughters Jessica and Naomi Hendel are full of good-hearted tolerance and cheerful advice, like, "Write, mom, write!" I would like to say thanks to Mr. Jon Hendel for years of support. Finally, I would like to express my gratitude and love for all those who have encouraged and supported me along the way, including, but not limited to, Caitlin Alexander, Rev. Col. Dr. Thomas Ayers, Lynn Bell, Paul Brodeur, Kim Bunton, Lynda Cassanos, Connie Dirago, Helen Fosbery, Stuart Gartner, Dan Halpern, Patricia Hatherly, Rita and Myron Hendel, Julia Howard, Catharine Karas, Geoffrey Knauth, Drew Lawrence, Matthew Olszewski, Theresa Pinder, Chris Schelling, Jo Slatton, Komilla Sutton, Gerda Swearengen, Dana Tierney, and Arthur Wooten, with special love and thanks, and an extra hug, to Dani Antman. To Lorine "Granny Bee" Adkerson and Judy Poff, wherever you are in the unified field, my love and thoughts are with you.

INTRODUCTION

The future breaks over the present like surf on a pebbly beach. The past washes in, too, a different tide under the same moon, and just as loud, swelling, and immediate. Einstein's Theory of Relativity tells us that time, by its very nature, isn't constant; it contracts and expands with the frame of reference. But the fluidity of time isn't confined to the dry strictures of science. Everyday life in all its messy intimacy abounds with examples of time dilation and relative simultaneity. Those examples are often so commonplace as to be unremarkable: absorption in a task that makes an hour seem like five minutes, or boredom that weighs on the ticking hand of a clock and drags it backward. Less ordinary incidents of time's sinuousness are still common enough not to be shocking: a vivid dream of an old friend, followed by that friend's appearance at the door; the knowledge of who is calling when the phone rings, but before it is answered; a wife's deep forebodings of a threat to her husband the day before he suffers a car accident; the inescapable sweep of déjà vu on setting foot in a place that we know logically we've never visited before, yet which feels as familiar as if we'd lived there for years. There's even an increasing cultural play with the concept of incarnational memory, and knowing specific details about the past that aren't plucked from Hollywood movies or from historical texts, as the best-selling books of the Dalai Lama and Dr. Brian Weiss and the TV show *Crossing Over with John Edward* demonstrate. Furthermore, reincarnation and prescience connote spirit, that nebulous realm larger than matter, and suddenly our ordinary domestic experiences don't seem so pedestrian.

So we have the sense that time isn't linear, and the larger implications of that are seeping into popular consciousness. Still, we grapple with it. We are caught in a conflict between the deeply embedded, orthodox, old-school "scientific" notion that the universe is a grand machine which can be entirely described by physical law that is, in turn, reducible to mathematical equations, and the inescapable presence of prescience and intuition, faith in divinity, our regular and real experiences with a linear-time-collapsing magic that escapes the bounds of law and logic. As human beings that both think and feel, we are caught in a paradox. On one hand, science is a true description of the world; it works; and it has greatly enhanced our lives. That I can curl up at night with a good mystery and read by a 100-watt incandescent bulb is both a pleasure and a benefit. When my younger daughter is screaming with an earache and the amoxicillan sets to work healing the infection, I am more than grateful to modern medical science. Yet there is also truth and reality in the mystical action of spirit, and spirit affects human life constantly. We all encounter it, from prayer and meditation to the forementioned experiences of time's inconstancy. We can't get away from spirit, with its many facets. We've been obsessed with it since we shed fur, stood upright, and picked up charcoal to sketch on cave walls. It is madness and ecstasy and creativity, god and demon, prophetic knowing and total surrender, as much and as necessary a part of us as our liver or brainstem. Perhaps it is this very mysticism that defines us as human, set apart from all other animals.

Turn on the television and examples of our fascination with mysticism—with the paranormal or the supernatural—abound. *Bewitched, The X-Files, Providence, Charmed, I Dream of Jeannie, Joan of Arcadia, Pet Psychic, Sabrina the Teenage Witch*, and my daughters' favorite, for reasons of a certain undead blond bloke, *Buffy the Vampire Slayer*, are just a few. The wonderful *Harry Potter* books enchant children and adults alike. In film, there are *Ghost, Field of Dreams, The Sixth Sense, Dragonfly*, and too many others to list. We are flooded with images of a mystical spirit that shatters linear time at work in the world. These images have persisted into modernity, surviving the occupation of the forces of mechanism and the sanitization imposed by the age of reason, because there is truth in them. Some part of us knows this, knows that they are the essence of humanity. But we wrap up the images in fiction because we aren't entirely comfortable with spirit. We want to be able to package it, tidy it, prettify it, control it—to deny it, if it comes too close to where we live.

And where we live, in the early twenty-first century, is a culture still convinced of the inviolability of classical, Newtonian physics: that is, a clockwork and deterministic universe that operates in orderly linear sequences that can all be expressed in tidy equations. This model crumbled in the face of Einstein's energy=matter physics and of quantum theory's indeterminism, but somehow, the newer precepts of quantum physics with its probability waves, field theory, and uncertainty principles, and their radical implications, are only slowly permeating our collective consciousness. Science as it is typically formulated is a closed system, with rigid boundaries. It's entirely opposed to spirit, prophecy, magic, mysticism, the paranormal, the supernatural, etc. I am using "science" in a large sense, referring to traditional "hard science": physics, chemistry, biology, astronomy. This collective sets itself up in mocking opposition to mystical experience, and it has infected our culture so thoroughly that we can only whisper about our paranormal experiences, while glancing over our shoulders for the thought police, or join religious, spiritual, or "New Age" groups that are seen as alternative and are tolerated because people need an outlet for their imagination and for their yearning for a big parent in the sky.

This schism has had huge cultural consequences, as we have lost some essential piece of our humanity. In seeing life as reducible to parts whose interactions are local and machinelike, we've given up our unknowable divine spark, our immortal soul, our open-heartedness. We narrow down our notion of reality to contain it in a small package, and we can't simply be with the vastness of what is. Pure determinism, unsoftened by an acceptance of paradox and mystery, creates an anxiety that incites us to vanquish the unknown and turn it into what it isn't—the known. I see this fundamental anxiety as part of why the family unit is disintegrating, unspeakable violence tears through our society, pollution is poisoning our beautiful, precious planet—and why we are suffering unprecedented rates of cancer and immune system disease. It even has something to do with the horrific acts of terrorism that devastate lives across the world, because out of the schism and the anxiety it produces comes fragmentation and intolerance, which blocks access to the full spectrum of our own, and other people's, humanity. Intolerance therefore promotes an emphasis on purity as being that which is like us, and the necessary end of a fixation on purity is terrorism.

So we've had to choose between a reductionist view of ourselves as mere biological machines in a mechanical universe, which devalues the bonds of love and kinship and reverence, and a mystical view which acknowledges the invisible, transcendent, and even mysterious core of our unified beingness, but which is scorned as medieval. We're caught in a chasm between orderly structure and unbounded mythos. We've been unable to find some meaningful bridge between the magical and the mechanical, a bridge built of the science that we know works in practical, demonstrable ways. We've been unable to unify reason and technology with love and incantation, which we have also experienced as true, if unfathomable, and we've all suffered for it. We're a fractured, schizophrenic culture. Modernity has brought us proficiency without the coherence, within the individual or between individuals, that is true freedom.

At least, this has been the case until the last decade or so. Suddenly, something exciting is happening: science is catching up with mysticism. A recent independent film called *What the #$BLEEP*! Do We Know?* has even brought this to the popular media. From physics to biology, an understanding of nature is emerging that links science with the very essence of prophetic spirituality. Quantum physics and radical new biological experiments prompt a deeper inquiry. This inquiry yields the same insights that seers have been conveying for millennia: an individual is a focusing of dynamic energy fields through consciousness, and that consciousness is unitive. We are all one in the great Oneness of the universe. As American mystic and prophet Edgar Cayce said, "Life and its expressions are one."

In the face of this unity, time and space fall away, for both mystics and scientists, validating the subtle experiences we more ordinary folk have. "Reality" occurs in a moment of here–now, and consciousness is inextricably involved. Anything that ever can happen, ever will happen, and ever has happened, anywhere, is contained within this divinely harmonized moment. Prophets like Edgar Cayce, whose vast body of work insists on the oneness of life from the macroscopic to the microscopic, are able to obtain information from within the unity to guide people. Cayce found this information in the Akashic Records, and spoke of going to a hall of records and obtaining a "book of Life" or a "book of remembrance" which was "God's book." He spoke of the Akashic Records "written upon the skein of time and space" many times in his thousands of readings, giving explanations and descriptions that, upon close reading, resonate with the "morphic field" postulated by English biologist Rupert Sheldrake and the "ten–dimensional mind domain of the Tiller simulator" as conceived by physicist William Tiller. Perhaps it's better written that these newer notions sound like Cayce's Akashic Records, because Cayce gave his readings decades before the morphic field was hypothesized, when quantum physics was in its infancy and field theory was not generally publicized.

As much as Cayce's work has been studied, and there are many dozens of books on Cayce and the readings, it's important to re-examine his work as science and modern life continue to evolve and bring us to new understandings, questions, opportunities, and impasses. There is great familiarity with "channeled" psychic work today, but Cayce's psychic readings are remarkable for their completeness and coherence. Cayce left behind a large, well–organized body of work that has been documented, cared for, and made available to the public for inspection. The readings are also unusually practical. They offer concrete advice on a variety of subjects, as well as the geological predictions that have become typical of channeled material, and information on mysterious subjects like Atlantis and humanity's distant past. The fullness and groundedness of the Cayce readings give them great importance—especially when so many of his suggestions and predictions culminated in healing and truth. Furthermore, the Cayce readings speak to an emphasis on wholeness and integration that is urgently needed in our fractured world.

There are a few scientists whose ground–breaking work is es–

pecially relevant in the context of Cayce, mysticism, and healing the rift between science and spirit. Dr. Rupert Sheldrake is an iconoclastic biologist who has written about morphic resonance, a process by which the probability that something will happen again after it has happened once is increased. Dr. Sheldrake wrote the book *A New Science of Life* to put forth the argument that morphic resonance specifically affects morphogenetic fields, which delineate the way developing systems like embryos come into being and evolution happens. He claims that through morphic resonance, "the morphogenetic fields of all past systems become present to any subsequent similar system; the structures of past systems affect subsequent similar systems by a cumulative influence which acts across both space and time."[1] His book *The Presence of the Past* explores this premise more, and discusses further the memory inherent in nature: "Memory is inherent in nature . . . Natural systems . . . inherit a collective memory from all previous things of their kind, however far away they were and however long ago they existed."[2] In his book *Seven Experiments that Could Change the World*, Sheldrake grounds his ideas firmly into the experimental heart of science, suggesting repeatable experiments that could "open up science, both in practice and in theory."[3] In particular, Sheldrake is interested in paranormal phenomena that traditional, mechanistic science can't explain and doesn't want to, such as the invisible connections pets have with their owners and the nature of the extended mind, that uncontained consciousness that "reaches out of the brain to touch everything it sees."[4]

Dr. William Tiller, who taught at Stanford University for over thirty years, explores quantum physics in relationship to consciousness, especially the mind's intentionality and the subtle energies of the body. He formulates the Tiller Model, stating: "My working hypothesis is that we are primarily elements of spirit, indestructible and eternal and 'multiplexed' in the Divine. As such, we have a mechanism of perception which is a ten–dimensional mind domain . . . We are spirits having a physical experience."[5]

Scientists Sheldrake and Tiller articulate their findings differently than Cayce. Whatever the language, common traits emerge. The Akashic Record is made by a whole unit of person, a "bodymindsoul" which Cayce called an "entity." The morphic field and ten–dimensional mind domain are holistic in like manner. The Akashic Records are evolutionary, revealed for evolutionary purposes; just so with the morphic field and ten–dimensional mind domain. All are relational with the universe, transcending time and space, and form–producing. And, ultimately, all are sacred, involved with the divine.

The narrative that follows uses my own life experiences as a springboard for exploring the similarities between the Akashic Records, as described in Cayce's voluminous and meticulously documented readings, and the current scientific models of the morphic field, the quantum domain, and superstring theory. I relate personal anecdotes because it is a part of my premise that the personal and intimate is a door that opens directly onto a view of both science and spirit, which are united. The polarization of formal science and daily human experience, or mystical experience and daily life, is unnecessary, misleading, and even dangerous, as polarities often are. Autobiography and lab reports aren't so far apart. The work of Rupert Sheldrake and William Tiller are also investigated. What finally makes these related ideas so relevant and important is that, in the sense of all life being one, the Akashic Records, like the morphic field and quantum domain, permeate everything. They aren't "out there," but flow through each of us. We live and have our being within them. They are all versions of the larger unifying field that some call "God." Because we aren't separate from that field, we can learn to access the Akashic Records for the improvement of our lives and the lot of humanity. We can build the necessary bridge between reason and magic, first within ourselves, so that we embody the unity of logical structure and mythic magic, and then in the larger culture, so that we can begin to heal some of the problems that plague our world.

Cayce related that the information for his readings comes "From the universal forces that are acceptable and accessible to those that in earnestness *open* their minds, their souls, to the wonderful words of truth and light." (254-83)* Knowing where current scientific theory and experiment merges into the mysticism of words of truth and light can greatly aid in opening our minds, given how our minds are influenced by the modern scientific paradigm. Science can finally be reconciled with spirit. Science can be one avenue in to a personal experience of the divine, along with prayer and meditation, prophecy and revelation, and poetry and music and art. We can directly, palpably, experience what Albert Einstein meant when he wrote, "All religions, arts and sciences are branches of the same tree. All these aspirations are directed toward ennobling man's life, lifting it from the sphere of mere physical existence and leading the individual towards freedom."

---

*During Cayce's life, the Edgar Cayce readings were all numbered to provide confidentiality. The first set of numbers (e.g., "254") refers to the individual or group for whom the reading was given. The second set of numbers (e.g., "83") refers to the number in the series from which the reading is taken. For example, 254-83 identifies the reading as the eighty-third one given to the individual or group assigned #254.

CHAPTER

1

I was driving home to Manhattan with my two young daughters one evening after a visit to my mother in Connecticut, watching the dotted white lines on I–95 roll by and ruminating on how the visit had been peaceful. My mother and I had found a compassionate connection to each other and enjoyed our time together. It didn't often happen that way. My mother and I had a troubled relationship filled with old disappointments, hurts, and bitter regrets. She was a teenager and a high school drop-out when I was born, and my father, though charismatic and intelligent, was a dark and difficult man, an unfaithful alcoholic with a wild temper. He was an enlisted man in the Navy and was transferred around the country frequently, which meant chaotic uprootings. My mother had a sparkling, intelligent spirit and natural optimism, gifts as a painter and artist, and a deep love for nature, but her life had not been easy. She was the third child in four of itinerant farm workers who divorced, and thereafter her own mother struggled to support the children. My mother had forays into medication that didn't work well for her, agoraphobia, a suicide attempt, and hospitalization. I often felt as if I were taking care of her when I was young. I yearned for more support and understanding and approval from her. She felt already stretched, as if too many burdens like hard blows had been forced on her—and her feelings were valid.

When I had children, the path between us smoothed. I understood better the deep responsibilities that had crushed my mother, and she understood my life as a parent better than she had ever understood me traipsing off to college or braving the big, dangerous city to set up a life with my Jewish husband. My mother loved my laughing, blue-eyed older daughter, and the feeling was richly reciprocated. Four years later, a feisty second daughter was born, this one with dark hair and dark eyes, like my mother and me. My mother enjoyed the little one's mischievousness. At the time, my husband was working hard to establish himself in his profession. When he traveled to his company headquarters in Chicago, I went to visit my mother in Connecticut.

As I returned to Manhattan, I contemplated the visit. Perhaps some highway hypnosis set in. My older daughter was curled up in her seat belt, dozing, and the six-month-old little one was asleep in her car seat. The radio played soft rock at a low volume. In the midst of this pedestrian moment, I was seized by a transcendent feeling. It swept over me in a vast, irresistible wave, gilding everything in the car with the hue of higher consciousness. I was possessed of a knowing, all at once, but it wasn't linear. It was circular and complete. I knew that I had to treasure the rapprochement with my mother—because it was sweet, but it wouldn't last. I knew with an ache that we had only a few months left to share this rare accord. Something would happen that would end it. Something would happen that would make it impossible for us to recapture the gentle, peaceable connection. I knew that we would be estranged, that I would go years without seeing her. Then I had a vision of her at the end of her life.

I was shaking and my heart was sputtering so loudly that I almost pulled the car over to the side of the road. I managed to breathe deeply and slowly realized that I had never lost control, never lost my calm. Part of me kept driving and watching the road while another part of me intensely experienced a supernatural knowing. The part of me that maintained vigilance wondered what it meant and if it was real. The other part knew, beyond reason or doubt or belief, that what had transpired was real, true, and accurate.

Indeed, life has played out in a way that has validated most of that unexpected foreknowing. A few months after that vision, my father, who was divorced from my mother, was diagnosed with lung cancer. His death, as his life had, brought out the worst in everyone involved: deceit, hate, cruelty, selfishness. In the end, heart-broken and spiritually sickened, I walked away from what I felt were toxic acts of betrayal on the parts of my mother and sister, thoroughly estranged.

As of this writing, I hear that my mother is still alive, so I don't know if the vision of her at the end of her life will ripen into fact. I will have to wait and see. But the way the rest of the vision played out marked me. It taught me how concrete prescience is, and how solid its impact is in human life. Prophecy isn't vague and remote, like the nonspecific mutterings of a musky fortune-teller trying to hook in a gullible client with threats of danger and enmity. Perhaps some is, but in my experience, real prophecy is tangible and specific. It touches the most important parts of human life: relationships with loved ones, health, daily events.

I was not surprised to have this supernormal experience, and ultimately, not surprised at how it came true. At the time of this event, I was attending a school for hands-on or spiritual healing and pursuing a spiritual path that was based largely in meditation and study. I had ventured into a course of spiritual inquiry when I was in graduate school, when I began meditating, and a garden–variety clairvoyant sight opened. Rather, it reopened. I had seen stuff as a kid. In the way that misfortune and suffering leave gifts in their wake, my turbulent home life evoked extreme vigilance, and for me, the vigilance morphed into a second sight. It was practical, because it was about self–protection. My father was prone to erupting with rage and then beating us; it behooved me to figure out beforehand when he was about to explode, and then to make myself scarce. The colors wreathing around his head would tip me off. Muddy reddish–black clouds would curl around his face and chest. I'd feel a heavy pressure like a vise clamping around my own skull and throat. For me as a young girl, seeing auras always went along with body feelings, pressures or warmths or textures, and the physical sensations confirmed the visions.

I also saw flashes and columns of light, entities, and various cloudy forms and presences. Leprechauns appeared once after a tornado in Kansas, where my father was stationed at a naval air base. At least, I called them leprechauns. Whatever they were, they stood knee–high and they didn't leak emotions and judgments, the way regular people do. These leprechauns were different, inscrutable. Even as a little girl, I had the sense that they were beyond ordinary notions of right and wrong. They fascinated me but I kept my distance.

Sometime in high school, I shut down the sight. For me, as for many others, the logical rigors of geometry and the factual analysis of history and literature interfered with my perceiving that other, nebulous realm. The two worlds seemed sharply at odds— mutually exclusive, even. I relegated my old visions to the active imagination of a creative kid. However, in graduate school, meditating regularly, I began to feel and then to see things again. Older now and with the tools of education, I gravitated toward books, trying to understand the strange phenomenon. I read everything about clairvoyance and psychic awareness that I could find. One of the first figures who stood out in my research was American mystic Edgar Cayce. He had given thousands of psychic readings to individuals concerning their health, relationships, business affairs, karma, past lives, and future. He had accurately predicted wars and geophysical events like earthquakes. His readings presented a unified view of all force and all realms as one, as purposeful, as organically and intrinsically interrelated in a dynamic field of creative consciousness. This view gave his readings critical and immediate importance, even though Cayce died in 1945, because it's precisely the view that offers us hope and healing now. Moreover, most of these readings had been meticulously recorded, documented, and followed up. They had been studied for decades by people in all professions, and they were available to examine, which intrigued me and led me to research his work.

Edgar Cayce would loosen his tie and collar, take off his shoes, lie down, fall asleep, and then diagnose people anywhere in the world with almost one hundred percent accuracy. In his sleeping or trance state, Cayce's mind seemed free of the constraints of time, place, and conventional logic. He could pluck seemingly endless, and accurate, information from the past, present, and future. He could locate an individual anywhere, scan the individual's body, and read the individual for illness. He used detailed and medically accurate terms that far exceeded his eighth-grade country-school education—terms whose meanings he did not know and whose pronunciation tangled his tongue in his normal waking state. He recommended treatments and medicines that were cutting edge, for the time, or, conversely, that drew on old-fashioned herbs and antiquated remedies. When followed, his recommendations resulted in an almost total success rate.[1]

His readings encompassed the gamut of human disease, from colds to injuries to cancer to pregnancy. The readings included detailed information about the subject's emotional state, including secret guilt and despair, impatience and pessimism, doubt and selfishness. The readings accurately described relevant past physical or emotional traumas, and eventually, as his career as a "psychic diagnostician" progressed, they brimmed with references to past–life trauma and karma, world prophecies and global readings, and geological predictions.

Edgar Cayce's life didn't immediately proclaim his gifts. He was born on March 18, 1877, in Kentucky.[2] His father Leslie Cayce was a sociable schemer, a failed farmer who became a shopkeeper; his mother Carrie was an educated woman from a prosperous family. By all accounts, Cayce was an intense and inquisitive child, less interested in school than in fishing and playing alone in the garden with his imaginary friends. It's said that Cayce struggled in school, and that the first inklings of unusual powers glimmered when he fell asleep over his studies with his head on his book and woke knowing his lesson thoroughly. Thereafter, that was his preferred mode of studying. He liked Bible stories and held a deep reverence for Jesus. Even as a child, he was a serious, committed member of his church and prayed often, with love and sincerity. He also read the Bible from start to finish many times throughout his life. When he was twelve, he had a momentous, life–changing experience: He was visited by a shining angel.

The story goes that Cayce had been walking in the woods, praying and asking how he could be of service to the Lord. I imagine that the combination of reverence and nature lifted him into an exalted state, the kind of state where prayers reach God's ear quickly, and the response can be heard in turn. After his afternoon outdoors, Cayce went home, ate dinner, performed his usual chores, and then went to bed. He was awakened by a bright light like a sun which seemed to radiate through his room. A figure approached and told the young man that his prayers had been heard and would be fulfilled. It ended by telling him to "'Help the sick, the afflicted.'"[3]

It wasn't for many years, until after Cayce was engaged to Gertrude Evans, that his healing and diagnostic gifts appeared. In fact, he was stricken himself with a mysterious throat ailment that resisted treatment and interfered with his job. He was always an industrious man and had worked as a clerk in a bookstore, a shoe salesman, and a clerk at a printing company and department store. He was employed as an insurance salesman in his father's business when he lost his voice to a persistent, voice-crippling laryngitis, which necessitated a job that didn't require speaking. He took his first position in a photo studio, as an apprentice. He had a flair for photography and did well, though his voice remained at a whisper. Doctors tried to cure him, and then hypnotists, to no avail. Finally a mail–order trained osteopath and hypnotist named Al Layne grew interested in the case. He offered to hypnotize Cayce and to ask Cayce's unconscious self how to address the malady. Gaunt, high–strung, and ravaged with pain in his throat, Cayce agreed.

Layne led Edgar Cayce through his first psychic diagnosis, with Cayce himself as the patient. Under hypnosis, Cayce spoke normally, proclaiming, "The trouble we now see is a partial paralysis of the vocal cords, due to nerve strain. To remove the condition it is only necessary to suggest that the body increase circulation to the affected area for a short time."

With alacrity, Layne said, "Tell the circulation to increase to the affected area and to remove the condition."[4]

Reports of the incident say that young Cayce's throat first blushed and then bloomed crimson. Cayce's father was watching and loosened Edgar's tie. Cayce spoke again, directing Layne to provide the suggestion that the circulation return to normal and that Cayce awaken. Layne did so, and Cayce awoke and spoke normally for the first time in months.

Al Layne was a sharp man and was impressed with Cayce's cure. It occurred to Layne that perhaps Cayce could diagnose and prescribe remedies for other people, not just himself, and he pressed Cayce to try—arguing that Cayce might be able to help people. Remembering his transcendent experience with the angel and the angel's counsel, Cayce agreed. The first subject for whom Layne wanted a reading was himself. Layne had been troubled for years with a gastrointestinal ailment that doctors could not alleviate. Eagerly Layne hypnotized Cayce again, and took copious notes as Cayce prescribed a specific regimen of medication and exercise. When he awoke, Cayce had no knowledge of what he'd said, but his prescription worked beautifully. Layne was healed.[5]

Slowly, working first with Layne, Cayce began to perform regular diagnoses of sick people. In the beginning, people came to him, but it soon became apparent that Cayce could read subjects at a distance. He wasn't limited to reading sick people, either. Or to reading people at all. Early in his psychic career, the sleeping Cayce recommended a remedy that could not be found at any pharmacy, so Cayce went back to sleep and provided the recipe.[6]

For the early trance readings, working with Layne, Cayce insisted on secrecy and anonymity. He wasn't entirely successful in this aim. People gossiped, especially friends and the delighted families of the healed subjects, and there was a small newspaper article. Still, mostly, Cayce managed to keep a low profile. Cayce and Gertrude were married in 1903, and a week after their wedding, a more substantial article appeared in larger newspapers throughout Kentucky and Tennessee.[7] Layne was forced to close up shop and attend medical school, and Edgar Cayce was widely regarded as a "freak." Cayce and his wife returned to his wife's childhood home and her parents lent the young couple the money for Cayce to open his own photography studio.

Cayce continued to do readings with Layne, and was even tested by medical students, with an esteemed professor overhearing the diagnosis. The medical professor was impressed with the reading, declaring the diagnosis "flawless."[8] Eventually a team of doctors wanted to test Cayce, and led him through several sessions where he was asked to provide such information as the genders of unborn children, the contents of a sealed envelope, the contents of a wrapped and unmarked bundle, and diagnoses of patients. In all cases, Cayce was correct.[9] The medical doctors were perplexed and uneasy, but convinced of Cayce's powers, having documented everything. They publicized their results and some renown came to Cayce. He was introduced to celebrated individuals such as Thomas Edison and Nikola Tesla. The publicity backfired for Cayce as the team of doctors grew ever more aggressive in their tests and even stuck pins into Cayce while he was in trance. Cayce awoke with painful sores and vowed never to let himself be tested again. He had personally encountered the unease and even hostility with which "rational" science views the occult.

In researching Cayce's life, I was struck repeatedly by how human a story it is. Cayce had a wondrous psychic gift, and was reputed to be a kindly, spiritual man of remarkable devotion, but nothing about him other than that stood out to anoint him as special and different. It seems to indicate that psychic access is a human phenomenon, available to all of us. It doesn't require mutant apparatus like a tentacle on the head, or a miracle like the voice of the Almighty booming down from the heavens. It seems to have more to do with intention, openness, and sincere desire, as illustrated by Edgar Cayce. That is, the waking Cayce appeared to be an ordinary man. He was slim, stoop-shouldered, and bespectacled. He had a wife and eventually children. He smoked and indulged in fatty fried foods. He had successes and failures, and sustained the devastating loss of his second child, an infant son. He didn't quite understand how ill his son was and didn't turn immediately to his psychic source for medical advice, so he blamed himself. It's the kind of thing we all do: underestimate ourselves, forget to use our own gifts, see with 20/20 hindsight. Cayce went into trance and read for his wife just in the nick of time to save Gertrude, whose inconsolable grief at the loss of her baby son sent into her a terrible illness.

With a family to provide for, Cayce wrestled with the domestic concerns that confront all of us: food, clothes, rent, and bills. He was a hard worker and a responsible man, and sometimes he was flush with earnings. There were other times he couldn't afford a winter coat. Since he had a strange and marvelous gift with seemingly no limitations, there were those who urged him to use that gift for material gain. He was asked to read the stock market and racetrack results. Occasionally, against his own judgment, he let himself be persuaded. However, Cayce encountered bad luck trying to use his psychic gifts for speculation. Accidents and misfortune attended those people who tried to profit from his trance readings. Cayce himself would develop severe migraines. At one point, his psychic source went silent. Cayce understood that he was to use his gift to help people—not to speculate.

For some time, with his source silent, Cayce concentrated on his photography career. Eventually he was enticed into giving readings again, and a few doctors again referred some of their patients to him. Dr. Wesley Ketchum consulted with Cayce frequently, and even, in 1910, presented a paper about Cayce's abilities to the National Society of Homeopathic Physicians.[10] Dr. Ketchum's paper sparked fierce interest in Cayce throughout the medical community, and resulted in a *New York Times* article and widespread celebrity for the doctor and his psychic diagnostician. The fame thrust upon Cayce led him to make a regular and systematic practice of his psychic readings, in the interests of being available to any sick person who requested his help. His readings were given at regular times, in an office set aside for the diagnostic work, and were meticulously transcribed by a secretary. Medical notes, follow-ups, and correspondence were appended.

Cayce read for people in all conditions, with a huge variety of problems: from tuberculosis to inflammations of all kinds, pellagra, broken bones and wasted muscles, paralysis, unsuspected pregnancy, palsy, blindness, tumors, hypertension and high blood pressure, arthritis, glandular disorders, gout, psoriasis, tooth decay, asthma, migraines, cancer, multiple sclerosis—Cayce in a trance state read whatever was presented. The healing system presented by his psychic Source placed emphasis on four physical areas: circulation, assimilation, elimination, and proper diet. To assist the first three areas of body functioning, he often prescribed osteopathic and chiropractic adjustments, massage, castor oil packs, exercises, laxatives, and colonics. He cautioned against regular use of vitamins, preferring that the body derive its nourishment from food. Most often, the readings tailor dietary advice to the subject, but generally recommend fresh vegetables, fruit, seafood for its iodine content, and meats except pork. One woman, a forty-year-old clerk, asked Cayce to outline a diet. The reply: "That which is body-building, ever. Have fish at least twice each week, liver twice each week; sweets, not too much. Raw vegetables once a day, in some form have these once or more each day. Cereals, fruits and vegetables well balanced, these would be a general outline. Fish, fowl and lamb are the better of the meats, see?" (357-13) As a mother who prepares meals for her children and tries to teach those candy-loving rascals some basic rules of nutrition, I can't help but be impressed with this sensible, balanced diet that avoids the bizarre excesses of fad diets and food fashions. I could never convince my daughters to chow down on liver on a regular basis, which may not even be appropriate in our current chemical– and hormone–laden environment, but in a less toxic era, it must have been an excellent suggestion for building blood, body, and strength. I also appreciate the advice given concerning the way meals were to be consumed: in a calm, relaxed manner to avoid nervous indigestion.

As the advice for calm eating shows, Cayce's readings didn't address physical illness from a simple mechanistic viewpoint, but from the standpoint of the dynamic interplay of emotions, the thoughts, the psyche, and the physical body. Cayce's prescriptions take the whole being into account: "To be sure, attitudes oft influence the physical conditions of the body. No one can hate his neighbor and not have stomach and liver trouble. No one can be jealous and allow the anger of same and not have upset digestion or heart trouble." (4021-1) Cayce's Source saw all body systems as working interdependently, affecting each other with exquisite sensitivity. In reading 2212-1, for a woman who was psychically diagnosed as anemic, with lesions on her spine and resulting vocal cord inflammations, the Source says, "The complications of the conditions of the system will require treating of this body, and we must act to save both the mental force in the body and the physical body. These actions or the enlarging to these excess glands and lobes in the body, show as a condition to the whole body." In other words, no one condition can be separated out from the whole. A fine balance tunes the body. A disease in one organ relates to the condition of the entire body, and the whole must be treated.

Furthermore, recommends the Source, "We have first into the system, oxygen to act to the forces of the system, to stop the forces of the high pulsations and temperature in the body and soothe the whole system of the body from head to foot, by a gentle rubbing of the whole body . . . a gentle moving and soothing of the whole body, with mental suggestion, strong, to the body as it is in the state of sleep." This prescription of gentle massage and mental suggestion is typical of the Cayce readings, which usually don't suggest a magic bullet cure for disease. Rather, the readings offer a comprehensive treatment regimen. Cayce's prescriptions weren't quick and dirty fixes. They required time, effort, attention—and they worked. They worked over time, and they worked because mind–body–spirit is a unity, and to address the multi–faceted human being this way is to elevate the whole being to a higher, more desirable level of ease and health. In particular, and this comes up frequently in the readings, the mind's power can be harnessed for healing purposes.

For tapping into mind power, Cayce's psychic Source exhorts subjects to have a positive mental outlook. The famous phrase that recurs in the readings is "Mind is the builder." It occurs literally hundreds of times throughout the body of readings. A typical example occurs in reading 996-11, when the Source was being queried about Cayce leaving for Virginia Beach. "Mind is the Builder, and in the building is how each applies in the action that as is gained—for, as we find, every thought is as a deed, and—as given—may be made a miracle or a crime." Thought is actually an action, a deed with consequences and results. Because of this, there's an urgency about schooling the mind, about directing the thoughts productively toward peace, harmony, compassion, tolerance. Beginning another reading, the Source relates, "In giving an interpretation of the physical, mental and spiritual well–being of a body, in terms of a mental and spiritual reading—as we have so oft indicated, Mind is the Builder. The mind uses its spiritual ideals to build upon. And the mind also uses the material desires as the destructive channels, or it is the interference by the material desires that prevents a body and a mind from keeping in perfect accord with its ideal." (357-13)

In the Cayce readings, the role of the mind was essential, preeminent: an individual's mind controlled what he experienced in life, what happened to him, how his life unfolded. Cayce's Source went so far as to assert that this was a cosmic law: "Individual conditions arise by the intent or projection of thought. Thought the builder, or mind the builder. Remember those laws." (900–374) People are not passive subjects; each person is the author of his own life, karma, and evolution. Free will plays a huge role in shaping life—this life and future lives. Holding a spiritual ideal firmly in mind, each person can create a life of miracles filled with peace and love. Or, wavering and sliding from that ideal, a person allows his or her life to founder. In giving this awesome power and responsibility to the individual, the psychic Source presents each of us with a choice that goes far beyond the migraine or bronchitis of the moment, though the Source begins with that and aims to alleviate those painful conditions. Instead, we are given a choice with far-reaching and existential consequences: What will we follow, love or fear? Where will we place our attention, and how will we focus our intention?

CHAPTER

2

There's a place in the non-material realms that is blue. It could also be called a space, because it opens up and out endlessly, though it has a calm, orderly feel. It's arrived at through meditation—for me, who both receives unearned moments of grace like shooting stars and also has to work at things, years of regular meditation. I can't always get to this peaceful blue: my mind won't shudder into stillness, I haven't been disciplined enough in my meditations, or something else happens for me in the meditation. When, usually despite myself, I do manage to enter into it, I find it nourishing, expansive, and restful. It seems to encompass and unify the polarities of limitlessness versus structure and boundary, or, said another way, freedom versus containment. It holds some kind of an answer, not a verbal one but a tactile and emotional one that addresses the soul directly, to the issue posed implicitly at the end of the last chapter about the nature of choice if an Edgar Cayce can see into the future. This space is one of those psychic landmarks mentioned through the ages by mystics, and it's well-known in spiritual circles. It's usually referred to as "the ether," "etheric," or "Akashic," terms which I researched for greater understanding.

"Ether" is an old physics term referring to an energy which fills the fabric of space and permeates the entire universe: "The notion of a plenum embedded in the fabric of empty space is not new to science. During the 18th and 19th centuries, the ether was considered the all-pervading medium which would sustain light waves."[1] It was initially theorized because if water waves are conducted by water, and sound waves are conducted by air, then light waves must be conducted by something, and that something is the ether. The ether was thought to possess some peculiar properties, because it was stiff enough to conduct light moving at the high speed c, yet massive moving objects like planets passed through it without resistance. Also, the ether penetrated throughout all space. Naturally, physicists, those curious creatures, wanted to explore the ether and its weirdness. Since the ether is everywhere, it would be hard to isolate for experiment—like trying to work with a thimble-full of sea water when standing on the bottom of the ocean. To address this problem, an etheric wind caused by the earth's motion around the sun was postulated. An etheric wind, it was reasoned, should be detectable. However, the famous Michelson–Morley experiment in the 1880s failed to detect an etheric wind, which led physicists to rule out an ether as well, though it threw them into some puzzling contradictions. Then, in 1905, Einstein made use of the Michelson–Morley results, and his work decided the matter.

Nineteen hundred five was a glorious year for the twenty-six-year-old Albert Einstein, for physics, and, because science affects all of us, for the world. In that year, Einstein published three papers that transformed physics: a paper on the photoelectric effect and on light as discrete bundles of energy called quanta, a paper on Brownian motion and atoms, and a paper which presented the Special Theory of Relativity. It must have been a sweet time of validation for the young physicist. Our current cultural images of him tend to feature the great genius as an older gentleman with a shock of fluffy white hair, but at this time, he was young and a bit plump-faced, with a well-kept mustache and curly dark hair smoothed close to his head. He was not yet a professor. Indeed, Einstein had struggled with academic discipline. He couldn't get a university teaching job, so he was working at the Swiss patent office. He hadn't graduated well from his university, not because he lacked intelligence, but because he was a creative and original thinker who insisted upon the freedom to pursue his own ideas. Even as a teenager he had hated the rigid academic high school he attended in Munich, because it emphasized memorization and obedience over creative thought. He had quit that high school mid-year and joined his family in Italy, where his middle-class German Jewish parents were starting a business. After some months, he took an entrance examination for the Swiss Federal Institute of Technology. He failed the exam. He enrolled in a different Swiss school and finally entered the Institute of Technology in Zurich, where he was the only graduating member of his class who wasn't hired for a university post—which landed him, a young husband and father, plump cheeks and mustache and all, at the Swiss Patent Office. His career situation changed after his revolutionary papers.

It was the paper on the Special Theory of Relativity that employed the Michelson–Morley results to vanquish the notion of an ether. Instead of an ether conducting light, time and space themselves were proposed to have unusual properties. It takes a bit of reasoning to see why, and some of it is beyond the scope of this book. But it comes down to the way that Einstein's Special Theory of Relativity states that "The laws of physics are the same for all observers in uniform motion." When this theory is followed out in logic and equation, it turns out that space and time aren't the constants they seem to be, but the speed of light c is— and the constant speed of light, no matter what, makes time and space malleable. Moreover, space and time are merged in a smooth geometrical fabric, a four–dimensional framework that can be called spacetime. Gravity is an inherent property of spacetime, the curving of its fabric in the presence of matter.

We all accept Einstein as the last word, and according to my research, relativity has been well tested and isn't likely to be refuted, but there were dissenters: "Nikola Tesla, inventor of the alternating current generator, designed his devices based on a belief in an ether, and he argued quite vocally with the scientific community on this matter."[2] Tesla must have been on to something because many of his inventions worked and worked well, such as his mysterious tube lighting that drew energy from an ambient force field.[3] There are even photographs of a gaunt and stern–eyed Tesla wreathed in eerie streaks and swirls of lightning, like some ancient god. Also, it is known that the United States government confiscated his papers and sealed the contents of his estate,[4] so perhaps there is something not yet entirely defined, not entirely understood or tamed, about this notion of an ether. Perhaps an ether exists, but it has properties that science can't yet measure and quantify, with our current tools, just as the truths of the plasticity of time and space existed when Newton spied a falling apple, but hadn't yet been discovered. Something about the ether continues to intrigue scientists. It persistently crops up in physics, recently reworked as the zero point field, the field of tumultuous fluctuating energy in the vacuum, in that spooky arena of the tiniest particles in the microscopic universe, a field which discomfited the incomparable Einstein himself: quantum physics.

Quantum physics is creepy, intriguing, and usually counterintuitive. It arose as scientists grappled with understanding the fundamental building blocks of substance. They kept looking at tinier and tinier building blocks of matter and energy, more and more basic particles, to see what exactly lay at the bottom, at the very root of everything—what particle couldn't be divided or reduced further. Particle accelerators were built to smash up particles so physicists could watch what came out of the quantum wreckage. What they found, and failed to find, amazed them. In particular, they failed to find specific answers: they found a realm not determined by machinelike and calculable certainties—they found indeterminacy. This means that when they experimented with electrons orbiting within nuclei, and with those tiniest bundles of electromagnetism called photons, and with less well known fundamental particles called gluons and bosons, they observed a startling realm of probabilities, uncertainties, and spontaneity. Amazingly, a photon can be both a particle and a wave, at the same time, a both/and phenomenon which flies in the face of the certainty implicit in the clockwork universe. Because it can be a particle or a wave, its probable location can be figured out, but not for sure, unless calculating its momentum is surrendered. In some real way, the thing isn't even there: it's a probability wave. Because at its fundamental level it's a probability wave rather than a concrete thing, and it's both a wave and a particle, only the observer triggers a definitive state, by looking for it. In that looking, the observer "collapses the wave" and triggers something definite—so the observer is paramount to the whole equation.

Quantum physics gets creepier. At the subatomic level, even solid material objects dissolve into wavelike patterns of probabilities, because matter has a quantum field associated with it.[5] There's no way to say for certain, "This is a particle located at these precise coordinates and moving with this momentum." You can estimate the probability that the particle is located at a specific place, but the more accurately you do that, the more you surrender knowing the momentum. In fact, when you ask, "Is this photon a wave or a particle?" The answer you receive back is, "Yes!" Nothing is deterministic. Nothing is mechanistic. Challenging the absolute relativistic speed limit of c, the speed of light, particles even seem to affect each other instantaneously over vast distances—or over any distance at all—as articulated in Bell's famous theorem, "Reality is non-local," a concept at which Einstein himself balked.

To further defy relativity, upon magnifying a tiny region of space many billions of times, fierce and stormy fluctuations of energy are revealed. The vacuum isn't a void anymore—it's a seething sea of energy, and within it, innumerable vibrating particles wink into existence and then wink away again. As said previously, these fluctuations are called the zero point field. It seems to contradict the smooth geometry of relativity, because of the "frenzy revealed by such an ultramicroscopic examination of space (and time) . . . The notion of a smooth spatial geometry, the central principle of general relativity, is destroyed by the violent fluctuations of the quantum world on short distance scales."[6] So quantum theory, which has shown experimental proof, and relativity, which has also proven itself, seem to be at war.

This strange, frothing field of energy into which particles appear and disappear is the latest candidate for the ether, which has both scientific and mystical connotations—connotations which must be bridged for the healing of humanity and our planet. Modern life has led us into a crisis of fragmentation, and a way out of this crisis is to unify science and spirit. Quantum theory in general lends itself to mysticism because:

> **Quantum theory implies unbroken wholeness for three reasons. First, action is composed of indivisible quanta, and hence interactions between different entities (e.g., electrons) constitute "a single**

structure of indivisible links." Second, entities such as electrons can show differing properties (particle-like, wave-like, or something in between) depending on their environmental context. Third, entities that have originally been combined show a peculiar non-local relationship "which can best be described as a non-causal connection of things that are far apart." (This is the Einstein-Podolsky-Rosen paradox.)[7]

Unbroken wholeness is one of the central defining tenets of spirituality and of most religions, from the Jewish Sh'ma, "Hear, O Israel, the Lord our God is One," to the paradoxical unity of the Christian Trinity, to the Hindu concept of "the Vedic dictum 'Truth is one, sages call It by different names.'"[8] To ponder quantum physics is thus to be transported immediately into the realm of metaphysics. And the vacuum that is no longer empty space but is now steeped with energy and potential lends itself to comparison with the mystical ether.

In mystical experience, the ether is that first spiritual level of subtle energy matter interpenetrating gross matter. In this way it resembles the sea of fluctuating energy that is the zero point field, because the energy of the zero point field is everywhere, and it mutually interacts with matter. The subtle realm as a whole contains other levels or planes, such as the mental plane and the astral plane and the dreamtime, that nebulous and illogical place we inhabit during dreams, though I tend to think of the dreamtime, because it is so fraught with emotion, as part of the astral plane. The ether is a specific realm, perhaps better understood as a particular vibratory rate in the spiritual spectrum, like the color blue is a particular wavelength in the electromagnetic spectrum.

Mystics often refer to the ether. Cayce spoke of his ethereal or etheric body, which was suspended above his physical body during a reading.[9] In fact, Cayce on occasion would stop speaking mid-sentence, or even sit bolt upright, if a hand was passed over his solar plexus area while he was in trance. Evidently he needed a free-flowing connection between his physical body and his ethereal body in order to download information for his psychic diagnoses.

When the flow between the etheric and physical realms was unimpeded, Cayce was a conduit for the information requested of him. He spoke of traversing the other realm to read metaphoric books that contained all information about the person for whom he was reading. The books were not limited by time or space but contained the past and future lives of that individual in all places, and he called them the Akashic Records. For example, in reading 1223-4, given in October of 1940 for a thirty-four-year-old woman, the question was posed: "Are there any records of my appearances? If so, where may they be found?" She was inquiring about concrete historical records of her past lives, so she could verify them, a most understandable, and sensible, desire. The answer: "These as we find are not as material records, but are upon the skein of time and space—or the Akashic Records." Asked to give a life reading for a forty-one-year-old man who was an osteopath, Cayce responded, "Yes, we have the records . . . In giving the interpretations of that as we find recorded by the entity in the realm of time or space, or Akashic Records, many an interesting experience might be singled out for the entity that has made and does make for definite urges in the experience of the entity in the present." (1334-1) The Akashic Records contain experiences undergone in the realm of gross matter, but they exist through and beyond it. And the records show how the past influences the present. Past and present are merged together, as the etheric and physical realms are, holistically.

The origins of the word "akashic" lie in Sanskrit. A Vedic astrological text defines it thus: "Aakash means sky or that which pervades all space, and is usually called the colour of the gods . . .

Aakash is the celestial electricity that connects us to the source."[10] I didn't find a reference in the Cayce readings to the sweet blue space of my meditations, or a description of the Akashic Records as blue per se, but there is a wonderfully resonant reading exploring an incident in which Cayce saw himself "going to the hall of records, to the old man with the books. This time, however, he saw and felt himself to be a bubble traveling through water to arrive at the place where he always gets the information." (Report on reading 373-2) Sky and space are clearly evoked in this image. Water is blue because it reflects the sky, and a bubble travels through either liquid or air space.

When queried about this image in trance state, Cayce related, "To bring from one realm to another those experiences through which an entity, a soul, may pass in obtaining those reflections that are necessary for transmission of the information sought, it becomes necessary (for the understanding of those in that realm seeking) to have that which is to the mental being put in the language of that being, as near as it is possible to do justice to the subject." (254-68) In other words, the bubble experience was a translation that Cayce, and the others with him, could understand as beings who live in the material plane. Furthermore,

> To reach that record . . . as of coming into existence across waters, the very thought of those present that it becomes necessary that that which is to receive or transmit the information must seek . . . meant that, the psychic influences in their activity with or through the physical forces of the body, must in some manner pass through the necessary elements for arriving at or reaching the beginning or that point. With the amount of water that is more often thought than of ether, what more befitting than that in the bubble the seeking forces should guide themselves!
> **254-68**

Cayce's psychic source is noting the need to translate psychic or subtle dimension experience into symbols that can easily be grasped in the concrete terms and prejudices of matter. We are physical beings, consciousness inhabiting a body, feeling ourselves subject to the restrictions of time and of three-dimensional space during our ordinary lives. Typically, we experience time and space as linear and constant; we just don't move at speeds close enough to the speed of light to experience relativistic effects on a daily basis. Our mechanistic science reflects this bias, despite knowing it to be invalid. And because of these prejudices, we think it's necessary to seek outside ourselves for the knowledge contained in the Akashic Records. That's what those present at the reading believed, too—that the Akashic Records were somewhere out there and must be journeyed to. The "psychic influences" thus accommodated their belief with a "passage through the necessary elements." Water is more commonly thought of than ether, and water and ether have similarities in their vastness and ability to conduct, so water was the element chosen. Cayce is the one making the voyage, so he has an experience that makes intuitive sense to him. He travels in a bubble to the place where the Akashic Records are kept. This allows him to believe in the trustworthiness of the information he is retrieving.

Cayce goes on to highlight more clearly the parallel with the ancient meaning of "aakash" as that which connects us to the source, that is, God:

> Of what forces? The psychic or soul forces, that are akin to what? The Creative Forces, or that called God. So, the body in a symbolized form as the bubble arrives at a place in which there is kept the records of all; as signified in speaking of the Book of Life, or to indicate or symbolize that each entity, each soul in its growth, may find its way back to the Creative Influences that are promised in and through Him that gives—and is—Life; and finds this as a separate, a definite, an integral part of the very soul. Hence

symbolized as being in books . . .   **254-68**

"Him that gives and is Life" is the Divine Source, to which the "soul in its growth" finds its connection. "Book of life" and "book of remembrance" are terms that the readings use interchangeably with Akashic Records, and "life" conveys something of the kinetic energy implicit in "celestial electricity." Here also is evoked the evolutionary aspect of the Akashic Records, that they pertain to the soul's journey of connection, communion, and unity with God. The Akashic Records are evidence that, to loosely paraphrase Einstein, "God doesn't play dice with the universe"; the universe isn't ruled by randomness, chaos, and decay. There's a deeper, divine order underlying apparent phenomena. There is meaning and purpose.

Cayce frequently speaks of the Akashic Records as being "written upon the skein of time and space" and "spoken of as the book of life" or "book of remembrance." They contain everything, but Cayce relates only what is useful to the individual during a reading: "In giving the interpretations of the records as written upon the skein of time and space, called in some quarters the Akashic Records—these are chosen with the desire and purpose that this may be a helpful influence in the experience of this entity; enabling it to better fulfill the purpose for which it came into this experience." (2522-1) This orientation toward using Akashic knowledge for self-improvement bespeaks a paradox that runs through the records: they are spoken of as "destiny" and as written, which implies something ossified, and yet they are not rigidly set. They have a certain elasticity. In one reading, Cayce says, "Let's turn to what is that termed as the Akashic Record, or that which may be said to be Destiny in the entrance of a soul into materiality." (903-23) Destiny connotes something that cannot be changed. Yet he goes on to explain that "souls in their varied experiences . . . are again and again drawn together by the natural law of attractive forces for the activity towards . . . the development of the soul to the *one* purpose, the *one cause*—to be companionate with the *first cause!"* (903-23) Development is dynamic and requires change. In another reading, Cayce clearly states, " . . . Akashic Records, in that spoken of as the book of life. Thus we find the book of life for the entity in the present appears very unsettled." (3506-1) This observation implies that the book of life is in a state of flux, and so, further, it can be changed, rewritten. There is something vibrant and lively about these Akashic Records that abound with all knowledge. Cayce calls them "a living record." (1292-1) He also notes that "the records . . . are both old and ever new." (2144-1) They contain all time, and yet are timeless.

Cayce was queried about the Records a number of times during the readings, and he gave some lovely analogies to explain what they are and how they are made. One was a comparison to film: "As we find, the record as is builded by an entity in the Akashian Record is to the mental world as the cinema is to the material or physical world, as pictured in its activity." (275-19) The subject's history in the psychic realm is likened to a narrative story and a vibratory recording, as tenuous, yet as convincing, as the electromagnetic projection of moving colored images upon a screen. In another reading, he draws a poetic comparison combining the images of film and music, saying, "The records of time and space—present and future—are upon those films that lie between time and space, and they become attuned to those forces of the Infinite as the cells of the body become attuned to the music of the realms of light and space and time." (275-39) The concept of "attunement," which is a resonant process rather than an end-point, again implies that the Records can and do change, that they aren't carved in granite. And the idea is posed of time and space as related dimensions with the Akashic Records as a kind of membrane of life or memory or even consciousness upon them. The "music of the realms of light and space and time" hints at superstring theory, which attempts to reconcile Einstein's smooth geometrical fabric of spacetime with the wild, unpredictable undulations of the quantum universe by proposing that "everything at its most microscopic level consists of combinations of vibrating strands"[11] so that "the universe—being composed of an enormous number of these vibrating strings—is akin to a cosmic symphony."[12]

Superstring theory, in other words, says that the basic, fundamental stuff of the quantum world isn't a point–particle, but is a tiny looped string in motion, "in hyperspace wherein the fields of Einstein, Maxwell, and Yang–Mills fit together with great precision. A ten–dimensional universe, divided into our traditional four and an additional compacted six, forms the minimal set needed to generate this precision."[13] The string is fantastically minute, but it does extend into space, unlike a point. The string's rate of vibration, its resonance, and its pattern of vibration, determine what it is, what substance it forms. Earlier quantum theories held that each elementary particle species was its own thing, fundamentally different from the others. A boson was its own beast, as different from a photon or a gluon as a salmon is from an inkjet printer. Superstring theory brings some foundational geometrical unity to things, and it does so without violating either the uncertainty of quantum physics or the laws of general relativity. Strings are still subject to what's called quantum jitter—they move in ways that keep us from knowing precisely both where they're located and how fast they're going. And yet string theory does contain a plausible constituent for gravity, that much theorized and never seen particle the graviton, so it contains gravity, the local curving of spacetime that is the central feature of relativity.

Sometimes the Cayce readings do more than hint at scientific theory. Sometimes they use language that seems directly plucked

from physics. For example, Cayce elaborates on the film metaphor, saying: "Where are the records kept? Upon what are they
recorded? Upon the etheric wave in time and space. What is the
film that makes between time and space? . . . In this film is the
difference between the movement of the atomic force about its
center and the impression that is made upon those passing between light and heat . . . " (490-1) "Wave" and "movement of
atomic force" insinuate light, that is, electromagnetism. In another reading, Cayce again mentions light: "The records of the life
are made much as the emanation of light from any source. For
the light moves on in time, in space, and upon that skein between same are the records written by each soul in its activity
through eternity." (815-12) The concept of light's motion through
time and space suggests velocity, and thus the speed of light c
and Einstein's fabric of spacetime through which it moves.

These scientific evocations do more than explicate. They also
ground Cayce's extraordinary psychic gifts in the practical world
of experiment, analysis, and logic. For this reason, Cayce uses the
same film metaphor to reassure a thirty-seven-year-old singer
who seems to have questioned the existence of the Akashic
Records: "The entity should know that the record is as real as that
which may be indicated by that given off as light, for it goes on
and on upon the etheronic energies and is recorded upon the
film of time and space." (871-1) The Akashic Records are waves
just as light is. They are as real as light. Although light is a metaphor for goodness, God, high consciousness, enlightenment, the
soul, etc., it is also a physical phenomenon. And it is used in that
literal sense in the readings. Furthermore, time, space, light, and
motion are the basic units of nature examined by physics. Cayce's
psychic source suggests that the science behind clairvoyant
knowing is accessible. In one reading, Cayce claims that someday,
an instrument will be made for reading the Akashic Records
(443-5).

Cayce even uses scientific language to explain how the records are made:

> Not light years as the Akashic Records, or as counted by astrology or astronomy in the speed of the reflection of a ray of light; for as records are made, the Akashic Records are as these: Activity of any nature, as of the voice, as of a light made, produced in the natural forces those of a motion—which pass on, or are upon, the record of that as time. As may be illustrated in the atomic vibration as set in motion for those in that called the audition, or the radio in its activity. It passes even faster than time itself. Hence light forces pass much faster, but the records are upon the esoteric, or etheric, or Akashic forces, as they go along upon the wheels of time, the wings of time, or in whatever dimension we may signify as a matter of its momentum or movement . . . Time, as that as of space—as inter-between. That inter-between, that which is, that of which, that from one object to another when in matter is of the same nature, or what that is is what the other is, only changed in its vibration to produce that element, or that force, as is termed in man's terminology as *dimensions* of space, or *dimensions* that give it, whatever may be the solid, liquid, gas, or what *its form* or dimension!   364-6

This lengthy description, in the Cayce readings' sometimes tortured diction, again evokes superstring theory. The key terms are "audition," which connotes auditory resonance, especially in an old–fashioned usage, and "changed in its vibration to produce that element, or that force . . . whatever may be the solid, liquid, gas, or what its form or dimension," which says that a change in vibration makes for a change in basic substance. This goes to the heart of superstring theory, which says that the basic, subatomic stuff of the universe is tiny vibrating strings. The rate and pattern of the string's vibration determines what kind of particle it is, what substance it forms macroscopically. Physicists looking for a

grand theory that unites all the principles of physics in a symmetrical, elegant form have been confounded by the vast number of different particles in the particle zoo of the quantum realm,
but that multiplicity isn't an issue at all in string theory: "Matter
is nothing but the harmonies created by this vibrating string.
Since there are an infinite number of harmonies that can be
composed for the violin, there are an infinite number of forms of
matter that can be constructed out of vibrating strings."[14]

The Cayce readings are presenting their own grand theory of
unification, which has to do with evolution, integration, wholeness. It's this theory that rectifies the fractured quality of our
contemporary life, that gathers together the destructive shards
into a whole container. According to the readings, the Akashic
Records are woven into the very fabric of everything, from the
spiritual realms through the material realms down to the level of
strings and the turbulent quantum foam that is smaller yet. The
physical component of these psychic records is clearly indicated
in that they partake of time, space, light, and motion. There is,
however, another factor at stake, the very one that makes the
Akashic Records literally "the Book of Remembrance" and "the
Book of Life." That is, they are suffused with consciousness. They
are dynamic, resonant, alive. So is the universe, into its deepest,
most fundamental levels. Everything is integrated together
through spiritual consciousness. Cayce stated this categorically:
"of the records made—upon time and space from God's book of
remembrance—we find life, as a whole, is a continuous thing;
emanating from power, energy, God–consciousness, ever." (1472-1)

CHAPTER

3

I dated a marvelous young man in high school. He was thin with a wild mass of curly dark hair and eyes that crackled with intelligence, curiosity, and kindness. He had a crooked smile and a droll sense of humor that included keeping his grandfather's oddly unused tombstone—because his grandfather had the same name, and seeing the death date after his own name amused my boyfriend. He had a great sense of compassion and moral obligation, which he claimed came from his intellectual atheism. I always argued with him, because I felt that goodness in the universe was one of the signs that God existed, along with irony. He firmly disagreed. An atheist carried the true moral burden, he reasoned, because there was no reward waiting in the sky. It was one of those points we never resolved between us, and there was room in our relationship for disagreement. My old boyfriend espoused tolerance the way other people revere Jesus, the Buddha, or the Knicks.

My boyfriend's salient characteristic, which I loved best about him, was his genius. That word gets bandied around until it loses steam like a child's top running out of spin, but it meant something applied to him. He was a true, inventive, creative genius. In calculus class while the rest of us were wrestling with the meaning of derivatives, he sat in the back of the room, chewing on his lip and doodling on a pad, deriving Leibniz's equations for himself. For fun. He read everything, including obscure journals, on topics which interested him. He designed and carried out research experiments to satisfy his own curiosity. He was an amateur astronomer and owned a decent telescope which we set up in his back yard, on nights he deemed less stricken with light pollution. We'd catalogue Messier objects, celestial objects visible with a small telescope and codified into a list between 1771 and 1784 by French astronomer Charles Messier. My boyfriend cross-referenced the Messier numbers with their New Galactic Catalogue designations, and he took notes. He was meticulous and precise. He was also diversified in his scientific interests. He owned a microscope which we used to examine all sorts of things, from tidal pool water to substances that were not G-rated. Years after we'd gone to college and split up and I was married with children, I heard an anecdote about him through the grapevine. He had decided to learn languages other than our old high school French, and he would buy a tape set, listen to it, watch some videos in the language, and then speak with extraordinary fluency, like a native. I believed the anecdote, because his was that kind of unbounded intelligence.

My youthful boyfriend taught me a lesson that has stayed with me all these years. He taught it by embodying it, not by lecturing. Simply put, it's that science is great fun. Science is about the play of curiosity, and imagination, and discovery. It's about the questions that pop into your head when you start to really look around at the world: How does that work? What makes that happen? Why? If one part is changed, how does that change the rest? What's here, and there, and underneath it all? There's something sparkly and fascinating about science, something that can seize you and shake you like a terrier would a furry toy in its mouth. It's that intrigue that carries a real scientist through into the other side of science, its strictness. Because the rigors that come with real, professional science are crucial. The logical precision, years of education and training and research, disciplined methodology, and exhaustive analysis, if they aren't glamorous, are exactly what ground science. They are what imbue it with its immense power to change, even to define, our lives.

Those rigors, coupled with the curiosity and imagination that hook people into a life of science, make it a dynamic, developing enterprise. We've come a long way, baby, from Aristotle's notion that an object's natural state was one of rest, to Newton's clockwork universe, to our current messy quantum indeterminacy and the relativistic elasticity of time and space. Now we are in the crux of a paradigm shift to accommodate what science has revealed over the last hundred years. "A new view of reality is emerging in Western science, a view that recognizes an inherent connectivity or oneness of seemingly separate objects; a view that allows consciousness, ultimately our very thoughts, to directly interact with other minds or objects. This view is called the holistic paradigm."[1] This holistic paradigm is what unites mystic Edgar Cayce with the radical scientists who are reformulating science; it's a broadbased and flexible way of viewing the world that takes into account the global village, our interdependence as humans even in the midst of ferocious ideological schisms, our need to husband the Earth's resources with wisdom and fairness—that is, our most pressing, most up-to-this-moment concerns. There are other terms for the new paradigm. Fritjof Capra, author of *The Tao of Physics* and *The Web of Life*, agrees that "The new paradigm may be called a wholistic worldview, seeing the world as an integrated whole rather than a dissociated collection of parts,"[2] but prefers the term "ecological" to "wholistic," when ecological is used in a deeper way. "Deep ecological awareness recognizes the fundamental interdependence of all phenomena and the fact that, as individuals and societies, we are all embedded in (and ultimately dependent on) the cyclical processes of nature."[3] Perhaps there is a play in semantics here; ultimately, this concept refers to unity and wholeness, from the microscopic to the macroscopic level, from the individual to the cosmic.

As mentioned earlier, one of the striking attributes of the Cayce readings that makes them so relevant today is that they are marbled through with this holistic or ecological worldview that is slowly taking root in our culture. They operate out of a fundamental integration of spirit and matter, science and mysticism, the open sweep of love and the boundaries of structure. The Cayce readings don't prescribe magic bullet cures, because the body is seen as completely integrated with mind, spirit, and psyche. Because physical systems are interdependent, many, sometimes all, facets of the human being must be addressed for healing to occur: The human being is a psychosomatic unity. Mind, body, emotions, spirit, psyche, and relationships cannot be separated out from each other, except artificially. Because of this fundamental unity, physical forces that affect individuals are seen as interwoven with spiritual or creative forces; Cayce goes so far as to talk about "the oneness of that force as may be manifested in the physical world from the oneness of all Universal forces." (254-27) In the holistic paradigm, as the human entity goes, so goes the universe—the parts are indivisibly integrated into a whole, with a creative Source that permeates everything.

The universal forces spoken of in the Cayce readings evoke quantum physics and string theory in ways already discussed, and vice versa, but physics isn't the only science to demonstrate the new holistic paradigm. Biology has also come around with its own holistic theories. One of the most arresting of these is the theory of morphogenetic fields and morphic resonance, as espoused by British biologist Rupert Sheldrake.

When my daughters read about someone in a book, they immediately assume that he or she is dead. It seems to be a common assumption. And while Einstein and Cayce have passed over, Rupert Sheldrake is very much alive, at the time of this writing. He even sent an e-mail to me suggesting a related book and wishing me good luck with this book, when I visited his web site and e-mailed him. It is devoutly to be hoped that he will continue for decades to come, producing books, lecturing, and provoking thought and debate, as he has done since his book *A New Science of Life* came out in 1981. At the publication of that book, Sir John Maddox, emeritus editor of the scientific journal *Nature*, wrote, "This infuriating tract . . . is the best candidate for burning there has been for many years."[4] Naturally, I think that any book that stimulates this kind of rabid response by the establishment is worth examining. There just might be some truth in it that orthodox fundamentalism doesn't want to examine and admit. New ideas usually seem to meet with fury and contempt—the unbalanced emphasis on purity, again, that fragmentation leads to—before the ideas reach a certain critical mass and widely inform human consciousness.

In *A New Science of Life*, Sheldrake "proposes the existence of subtle, hyperspatial 'morphogenetic fields' which guide the formation of matter or living systems. These fields are further strengthened by the physical manifestation they help form, thus making it easier to repeat creating the physical form . . . This field is non-local and hyperspatial in its nature and can be likened to an 'etheric' or 'spiritual' form."[5] Sheldrake starts with the premise of living organisms that are more than the sum of their parts, a clear departure from the pervasive paradigm of the machine.

From this premise comes the idea that living organisms are organized by invisible fields, that is, the morphogenetic, or morphic, fields that have measurable physical effects and that operate across time and space. These fields are a kind of memory in that "the morphogenetic fields of all past systems become present to any subsequent similar system; the structures of past systems affect subsequent similar systems by a cumulative influence which acts across both space and time."[6] Sheldrake gives the example of a substance crystallizing faster after it has once crystallized. The first episode of crystallization will take the longest, because there is no precedent, no morphic field to guide its development. Having once achieved crystallization, the substance then is associated with a morphic field which will be accessible to that substance ever after, and anywhere. And the morphic field will influence that substance to crystallize in the same way each time it crystallizes. Sheldrake calls this the "theory of formative causation." "Causation" comes from the way these fields serve as blueprints or templates for form and behavior. These fields are the agency through which form comes into being.

Sheldrake has been called a crackpot because of his radical theories, but his intellectual pedigree can't be faulted. He studied at Cambridge and at Harvard, earned a Ph.D. in biochemistry at Cambridge, and became a fellow at Clare College, Cambridge, where he was Director of Studies in Biochemistry and Cell Biology until 1973. He journeyed to India to work on crop research, and eventually lived on an ashram there, which is where he wrote *A New Science of Life*.

In this book, Sheldrake begins with biological phenomena that aren't easily explained by mechanistic theories. That is, not everything that we observe happening in bodies around us can be defined by the cut-and-dry mechanical processes of traditional biology. There are cracks in the container where observable phenomena that aren't mechanistic seep out, and Sheldrake in quires into them. For example, new structures appear in biological development which can't be explained by what's already present in the egg at the outset. That is, there's no leg present at the moment an egg is formed, and yet a fertilized egg will produce a child with two legs for hopping and skipping, unless something goes terribly wrong. Or look at the mush found inside an acorn. By some seeming magic, that mush develops into a mighty tree! How is this possible? It's sort of glossed over in traditional biology. But it leaves room for Sheldrake to entertain non–mechanistic ideas. Everyone can see that it happens; perhaps there is a field of influence at play here?

A second phenomenon is that developing systems regulate themselves, that is, "if a part of a developing system is removed (or if an additional part is added), the system continues to develop in such a way that a more or less normal structure is produced,"[7] and examples are given of embryos such as a dragonfly embryo. A dragonfly embryo will continue to develop into a fully formed dragonfly, only smaller, if part of it is removed during embryonic development. Other embryos can do the same thing. It's a counterintuitive developmental quality. In the mechanistic view of the world, removing a part of an embryo during development should deform the embryo, leave it without a major organ or limb. This doesn't always happen, which isn't thoroughly explained by traditional biology.

A third phenomenon is that organisms can regenerate damaged structures, such as when a newt loses an eye lens, it grows a whole new one, or, if a child under the age of eleven years loses a fingertip, that fingertip will regenerate.[8] Regeneration of body parts fascinates scientists, medical doctors, and people who have lost limbs or eyes or suffer from organ disease. How does it happen, and can it be prompted? There is great healing potential in figuring out how regeneration works. Thinking outside the box is essential here so we have the capacity to improve the quality of millions of lives.

A last, nebulously explained biological phenomenon that Sheldrake mentions is that organisms reproduce, that is, they send out a part of themselves which miraculously becomes a whole new organism. There's something mysterious and magical about reproduction, whether it occurs when a yellow dandelion wafts out a piece of fluff or when a male ejaculates. Traditional mechanistic biology states that these phenomena happen, but it doesn't explain exactly by what means they work. There are statements made about chemical processes, but that seems pallid and lacking in substance, as if it were tossed out only to further the credo of pure mechanistic determinism. "They must have a mechanistic explanation so they do have one," goes the thinking. But what exactly prompts those chemical processes? What spark makes the fire of regeneration or reproduction take place? Is the spark perhaps a field of influence?

In pointing out what's unexplained, Sheldrake also mentions parapsychological events, such as precognition, clairvoyance, memories of past lives, psychokinesis, and poltergeists. These phenomena are dismissed with much eyeball rolling by traditional, mechanistic scientists, but too many of us have experienced them firsthand for them to be dismissed with a cavalier gesture. Sheldrake notes that when fraud and superstition are taken into account, still "there remains a large body of evidence which seems to defy explanation in terms of any known physical principles."[9] Instead of refusing to examine these issues, science is better off asking how and why they happen. So, in methodically listing these biological and parapsychological phenomena which don't neatly fit traditional science, Sheldrake amasses the grounds for an argument against strict mechanism.

Theories of memory also play a role in Sheldrake's arguments. Personal memory is held by an individual of a species, but that's not the only kind of memory available, especially to people.

Sheldrake remarks on memory and the collective unconscious as formulated by Jung. Jung thought we inherited a collective memory, that its archetypes were universal and pre-existent. If so, this kind of memory works through time and space, in a manner Sheldrake terms "interactionist memory." It suggests that memory does not have to be stored physically in the gray matter of the brain. Memory is also an action or influence through time. In this view, memory is not locked up in the individual physical brain. It can move from person to person, accumulating, or between members of a species, collectively. It is a kind of field of experience and information that operates through time and space, and includes the instincts of animals. In this case, "mental phenomena need not necessarily depend on physical laws, but rather follow laws of their own."[10] This allows for nonmechanistic modes of operation: it breaks the box of the soulless clockwork universe. Sheldrake references other scientists such as zoologist Sir Alister Hardy, who proposed that the shared memory of a species "would act as a sort of 'psychic blueprint.'"[11]

Given the body of evidence suggesting that strict mechanism doesn't fit biology and related disciplines like psychology, Sheldrake has propounded morphogenetic fields and the theory of formative causation. He "proposes that morphogenetic fields play a causal role in the development and maintenance of the forms of systems at all levels of complexity . . . 'form' is taken to include not only the shape of the outer surface or boundary of a system, but also its internal structure."[12] In other words, the morphogenetic field not only establishes the instantly recognizable two-legged, two-armed, head-on-top-of-torso form of the human being, but also the organization and development of the human digestive system, and within that, the development and characteristic shape of the human stomach. He further broadens his theory by saying that all physical, biological, and chemical systems have morphogenetic fields, not just dragonfly embryos,

crystals, and human beings: "There must be one kind of morphogenetic field for protons; another for nitrogen atoms; another for
water molecules; another for sodium chloride crystals; another
for the muscle cells of earthworms; another for the kidneys of
sheep; another for elephants; another for beech trees; and so on."[13]
These fields are patterns of influence acting through space just as
electromagnetic or gravitational fields act through space. They
don't have mass or energy, but morphogenetic fields operate
widely and generally, within hierarchical patterns of complexity.
This means that the morphogenetic field of "dog" as a whole organizes the morphogenetic fields of canine embryological development, the canine reproductive system, canine ovaries, and
canine oocytes, in turn. The higher level field coordinates the
lower level ones. Sheldrake explains that the higher level fields
hold potential. They contain the "virtual form" of the final system, and the lower level forms act to fill out that final form.

Morphogenetic fields don't replace the action of DNA and
chemical and physical processes, they guide it. It's not an either/
or but a both/and scenario: Morphic fields work in conjunction
with genetic, chemico–physical processes to effect development
and evolution. Morphic fields become present to like systems
from the past and cause one shape to occur instead of another,
acting with known physical and chemical processes. They are the
"why" behind development: Why does this particular germ cell
in the zygote become a bicep muscle, and this other germ cell
become a toe? Because the morphic fields of past germ cells have
developed similarly. The way these fields guide development is
through repetition. The same kind of development toward an
outcome happens repeatedly, and that repetition strengthens the
morphogenetic field, making the same outcome more and more
likely. The first time an outcome happens is a result of chance, or
of "a creativity inherent in matter; or to a transcendent creative
agency"[14]—Sheldrake does take note of generative creativity in

the universe—but after that, it's the fact that it happened once that makes it likely to happen again, and then that it happened twice that makes it even more likely to happen the next time.

This reasoning makes enormous sense to me when I consider evolution. Chance, like buying the winning lotto ticket, could account for a few inorganic molecules colliding and sticking and becoming organic, but why would that happen again? And again? And start to increase until the earliest organic molecules became single-celled living creatures?

And then why would those single-celled living creatures become first multi-cellular creatures, and then fish, and then crawl onto land to build temples and churches? These questions have provoked a bitter dispute between two orthodox factions: creationists and evolutionists. Perhaps the answer is more subtle than either faction perceives. Perhaps the "intelligent design" of the universe is an unlimited field of intelligence and consciousness. We can think of this field as God if we wish. If we wish, we can also see this field of intelligence as containing within itself, and thus utilizing, biological fields of influence. That is, morphogenetic fields are the tool of this intelligent designer. In this way, morphogenetic fields can serve as the bridge between these two bitter opponents. In strictly evolutionary terms, here's the elusive sparking of life: After the first molecule became something more, there was a greater likelihood it would happen again. So it did, and then the likelihood was even greater. In the same way, after there was one one-celled organism, the probability increased that there would be another, because a field of influence had come into being, and that field of influence accumulates in strength.

Sheldrake explains the actions of the morphic fields by way of an analogy to resonance. Physically, resonance is a kind of enriching through vibration. It happens when a vibrating body is exposed to another body vibrating at a similar or sympathetic frequency. There is an increase in intensity, such as when I'm singing in the shower. The shower walls give my voice the soaring richness of Celine Dion's, which it usually lacks utterly, though that doesn't stop me from inflicting "My Heart Will Go On" upon my long-suffering family. This delicious acoustic effect is produced by the shower stall walls and the water vibrating in such a way that the vibrations of my voice are amplified and intensified. In similar fashion, morphogenetic fields resonate across space and time to meet similar bodies or substances or systems. Sheldrake calls this morphic resonance. It, too, "takes place between vibrating systems. Atoms, molecules, crystals, organelles, cells, tissues, organs and organisms are all made up of parts in ceaseless oscillation, and all have their own characteristic patterns of vibrations and internal rhythm; the morphic units are dynamic."[15] This description comes right out of quantum physics and string theory—and Cayce's readings. Moreover, Sheldrake clarifies, morphic resonance is three-dimensional, because it affects the form of a developing system, its shape in space, so that the system is guided to have orange butterfly wings or long nimble tentacles or broad green leaves, based on similar systems in the past. There is also a time dimension involved. By way of morphic resonance, the forms of similar systems from the past become present to a like system unfolding in the now.

This idea of fields without mass or energy, acting across space and time to guide developing systems by way of resonance and cumulative influence, is radical and heretical. It's no wonder that there were mutterings about burning Sheldrake's book. If we'd carried over the zealous methods of past eras for defending orthodoxy, Professor Sheldrake himself might have been burnt at the stake, as monk-scientist Giordano Bruno was in 1600. Fortunately, Sheldrake wasn't, and he expanded on his ideas in *The Presence of the Past: Morphic Resonance & The Habits of Nature*. Here Sheldrake really grabs orthodox science by the male genital glands: He questions the assumption of eternal laws of nature which can be verified through repeatable experiment. It's not the repeatable experiment part that Sheldrake challenges. He supports experimentation full-heartedly, and even wrote a subsequent book entitled *Seven Experiments that Could Change the World*, which takes as its mandate "a more open kind of science . . . a more open way of doing science: more public, more participatory, less the monopoly of a scientific priesthood" so that science is nourished "from the grass roots up."[16] To these ends, he suggests experiments that can be done by regular people who aren't professional scientists. But what Sheldrake does call into question is the assumption of eternal, immutable laws of nature that always work the way mathematical principles do. It's a wonder that no wild-eyed scientist in a white lab coat and black socks hurled a beaker full of explosives at Sheldrake for this one, because discovering nature's fundamental, unchanging laws is the charter of science as we know it.

In *The Presence of the Past*, Sheldrake looks at the origins of our assumption that nature is imbued with underlying and unassailable laws. He traces the history of scientific philosophy from its roots in Pythagoras' system of cosmic harmonic ratios and mathematical mysticism, through Plato's transcendent ideal Forms which are ideas in the mind of God, an eternal and rational order outside of time and space. In contrast, Aristotle proposed an immanent natural purpose of changeless souls, and eventually Thomas Aquinas synthesized Aristotelian immanence with the Christian mandate of development toward God's ends and perfecting the self in Christ. The Renaissance revived eternal Platonic Ideas, which were integrated into the budding science of that time. Copernicus and Kepler both espoused a Pythagorean apotheosis of mathematics and numbers, and Galileo went so far as to categorize mathematics with the absolute and unchanging, as opposed to the relative and subjective, in which realm lies human experience. In this way, Galileo created a dichotomy, separating human experience out from nature. This is the beginning of the great schism of modernity: the loss of wholeness and integration.

It was Descartes who then canonized mathematics as the embodiment of all truth. Ironically enough, and reminiscent of the young Cayce, Descartes came to his beliefs after a mystical experience with an angel: "When he was living in Neuberg on the Danube, on the eve of St. Martin's Day in 1619, the Angel of Truth appeared to him in a dream and revealed to him that mathematics was the sole key needed to unlock the secrets of nature."[17] I wonder if Descartes' Angel would have approved of this revelation being used, ultimately in the winding course of history, to discredit supernatural experiences—like angelic visitations. At any rate, thus inspired, Descartes proposed that, in the beginning, God set the world into motion as a great machine. So it has remained. With a reference to the Creator who would soon be erased from the equation, the French mathematician laid the foundations of the mechanism that has plagued our world in one form or another ever since. Isaac Newton then built on this by expounding permanent, fundamental laws of nature expressed through mathematical equations. Newton was himself a mystic, a student of alchemy, Kabbalah, and esoteric Hermetic knowledge, who saw God as the hidden force informing and binding the universe. For Newton, God filled the void. However, Newton's own reverence was extracted from his cosmology in the alembic of modernity, and "what was left was a world machine in absolute mathematical space and time, containing inanimate forces and matter, and entirely governed by eternal mathematical laws."[18] Here, then, is the source of our belief in a clockwork universe without magic or mystical spirit.

Having tracked down the historical origins of our belief in these absolute laws of nature, Sheldrake goes on to pose the question: What if nature operates more from habit than from law? The principle of the evolutionary universe, for Sheldrake, justifies this question. If the universe was created in an orgasmic shudder by the Big Bang, as current cosmology believes, and if the universe then grew and developed in time, then it isn't necessarily true that the laws of physics operated before the universe came into being. They might have; then again, since there was no universe for physics to work in, they might not have. However, after the Big Bang, the principles of physics started to function. They worked once, and then again, and then became habit, so deeply ingrained that the difference between habit and law is almost negligible. Therefore experiments yield reproducible results because the habit of, for example, Force=Mass x Acceleration, is so long-standing. The key to this line of reasoning is that the universe isn't static. It creates and it changes, that is, it is an evolutionary universe. Indeed, Sheldrake claims that "the concept of morphic fields developed in this book [*The Presence of the Past*] represents an attempt to understand such organizing fields in an evolutionary spirit."[19]

It's this evolutionary spirit that redeems us from the devaluation of seeing ourselves as biological machines, and we will go on to explore morphic fields in greater detail in the next chapter.

CHAPTER

4

My daughters and I own two horses which we board up-state, in the great little town of New Paltz, New York, where we have a plain, tiny, but much cherished cottage. These steeds of ours aren't fancy, and boarding rates upstate aren't astronomical, the way they would be closer to Manhattan. Still, horses are an extravagance for city dwellers. We've had to rearrange priorities and economize in other ways. It's been worth it, for my daughters and me, and not just for the glorious rides out on the hilly, wooded trails of this town, which is famed for the breathtaking Shawangunk Mountain Ridge. We've also met some extraordinary people in the barn at Coyote Ridge stable, and we've had experiences with Garfield the bay quarterhorse gelding and Loraygold the sorrel thoroughbred mare that have taught us about horses, animals, people, and life. Just as golf enthusiasts claim that golf is an analogy to life and that how you play the game is how you live your life, I would venture an argument that horseback riding reveals the true inner self and teaches life lessons. I mean, I liked walking around outside on a warm sunny day for eighteen holes with my ex–husband, but that erratic little white ball was *never* going to go where I aimed it. However, when I give Garfield a squeeze with my calves, his ears swivel back toward me and he picks up into a trot. As long as I communicate with him in ways he can understand, Garfield responds.

Usually he responds, that is. Horseback riding is a kind of partnership, a kind of dialogue. The human rider is the boss, but horses can have opinions. Certainly Garfield has opinions. And quirks. He's a burly, fourteen–year–old guy with the patience of a saint, ordinarily. My younger daughter throws a Western saddle on him and gallops him madly around the ring, riding with more daring than finesse. She gets a gleam in her eye just before she kicks him to go faster, and Garfield raced in his younger days, so he obliges her. He also takes extraordinarily good care of her. She started riding him a few years ago when she was seven, a dark–eyed, dark–haired, buck–toothed kid with a grin wider than her own head, tall for her age but skinny, and Garfield seemed to sense that she was little. When she was on him, he'd pick his feet up as carefully as if he carried a glass doll on his back. He'd eye me sitting on the fence, and trot to me if I called him. However, there are a few items he won't compromise on. He wants his rider to use a mounting block and not to jump on him; he hates having the stirrups twisted; and he doesn't want to be ridden at dinnertime. Garfield likes his evening bucket of feed. He wants to be left in peace to enjoy it. He'll ride all day before that, and he'll ride all night after that, but dinnertime is sacred. These are his idiosyncrasies; did he develop them, or did he inherit them, from his sire or the grandmother of his mother?

Loraygold, the mare, is a sweetheart, too. My older daughter takes extra time grooming her, partly because Loraygold is a tall, long-legged thoroughbred standing close to seventeen hands and so requires the time, partly because my older daughter likes to do things a certain way, and partly, I think, because the sweet-natured girl likes to coo at the pretty horse and have the horse whinny back. She brushes Loraygold until her coat shines like burnished copper and her mane is glossy and soft. My blue-eyed big daughter uses an English saddle and rides with the proud, erect posture of a queen. She likes the way Loraygold always lands on the correct lead and flexes her shoulder rounding a turn. We got a fair deal on this well-trained horse because she has a barely perceptible drag in her hindquarters which would make her unfit for extreme jumping, but we don't do extreme jumping. And as for the little drag, the vet who examined her for us said that an anti-inflammatory agent like bute would fix her up just fine.

Somehow, last summer when Loraygold went into heat, my daughters and I hatched the brilliant idea that we would breed her. Perhaps it was because I was pregnant at the time. We have zero experience in horse breeding, and, because we live in the city, we only get to see our horses on weekends, so it wasn't the most practical plan. It's also certain to cost more than we've allocated out of the family budget for our horses. It must have been me or my younger daughter who had the brainstorm, because it bears our signature: more enthusiasm than pragmatism, the kind of thing that often turns out well in the end, because God seems to enjoy innocent, if foolish, spontaneity. Connie, who runs the stable, chuckled and promised to guide us and to attend to the mare. She's a genial, grounded woman, knowledgeable in all kinds of animal husbandry. She takes in stray cats and dogs, birds that fall out of nests, and the baby rabbits we found in our garden when my new husband was breaking the ground for tomato plants. Connie owns emus and a farm full of pigs, chickens, and goats. Above all else, Connie knows horses. She's assisted the vet in many a delivery and enjoys it. She likes seeing the foals around the stable. She gave us a nod and it was a go.

Connie directed us to a friend with a big paint stallion named Paycos Pete. Petey had bred successfully many times, producing beautiful variegated foals with unusually sweet dispositions. Dutifully, if ignorantly, my younger daughter and I drove over to talk to the owner, a kind lady named Marcelle. She took us out to the pasture and had us admiring and petting Petey, who stood around patiently without a lead rope on. Marcelle explained to us that it was rare for a stallion to be so accommodating. She was proud that so many of his offspring inherited his sweetness. Marcelle is one of those passionate horse people who knows everything about her business of breeding horses, and she led us back indoors and gave us a lesson in the genetics of it. Loraygold is a thoroughbred and Petey a registered paint, and there were a few possible outcomes of the breeding. Petey is homozygous black factored, meaning that any foal he has will have black points, a black mane and tail or partial black mane and tail. He would never throw a chestnut, palomino, or red-factored foal. His foals would be bay, dun, buckskin, or black-and-white. Petey is registered as a Tobiano/Overo, otherwise known as Tob-Overo or Tovero. The outcome possibilities for a foal would be a Tobiano, in which white crosses the spine between the withers and the tailbone, typically all four legs are white and the tail is two-colored, with regular or distinct spots and more of a solid face that has a star or a blaze and no blue eyes; an Overo, which has no white crossing the spine but has a solid back, one or more dark legs, typically irregular white splashes, blue eyes, and perhaps a bald face; a Tovero, which is a combination of both, is mostly white, does have four white legs and white crossing the spine and can have blue eyes; or a solid, meaning bay, black, or dun, in Petey's case.

It was a lot of information that Marcelle presented to my

daughter and me. When she was finished explaining, Marcelle quizzed us like a school mistress until she was satisfied that we'd gotten it. She wanted to go into alleles and the actions of horse coat color genes, but my nine-year-old daughter made an aghast face at me. I hastily explained that we were expected back home. Eventually, almost two months later because Loraygold was finicky and turned her nose up at the stalwart Petey, Marcelle called with good news: There had been a breeding. She intuited it would be successful. A while later, ultrasound confirmed her hunch. So now we were waiting and wondering, what kind of foal would arrive?

This business of breeding and genetics is something we all know a little about, thanks to high school biology. We all know that a brown-eyed mother who makes a baby with a blue-eyed father will produce a brown-eyed child with one gene for brown eyes, from her, and one gene for blue eyes, from dad. This holds if the mom has two dominant genes for brown eyes. However, if she has one dominant gene for brown eyes and one recessive gene for blue eyes, there are more possibilities: she could have a brown-eyed child with a dominant gene for brown eyes and a recessive gene for blue eyes, or a blue-eyed child with two recessive genes for blue eyes. In fact, this happened in my case, where I have a dominant gene for brown eyes from my own brown-eyed mother and a recessive gene for blue eyes from my blue-eyed father, and I produced one daughter with blue eyes and one with brown eyes. Like my daughter's horse, I'm pregnant as of this writing, and we know it's a girl. My new husband has light eyes, more of an amber or golden green color than blue, and I'm guessing it's a recessive color, because I've seldom seen it. So, what color eyes will the new baby have? It will depend on the genetic lotto and on which genes for eye-color are dominant, the gene for brown eyes, the gene for blue eyes, or the gene for amber eyes. We all figure this way because of what we learned about

Mendel and his experiments in high school biology.

However, Rupert Sheldrake points out that this way of think-ing, or articulating the genetic process, is inaccurate and poten-tially misleading:

> What genes are known to do is to code information
> for the sequence of chemical building blocks in RNA
> and protein molecules. Thus they help to provide a
> detailed understanding of the way in which organ-
> isms inherit their biochemical potentialities. What
> they are *not* known to do is to code for morphogen-
> esis or for inherited patterns of behavior. They are
> not "determinants" . . . Many biologists are, of course,
> well aware that it is misleading to speak of genes "for"
> particular characteristics. Dawkins, for instance, has
> made it clear that if a geneticist speaks of genes "for"
> red eyes in the fruit fly *Drosophila*, he implicitly
> means that "there is a variation in eye color in the
> population: other things being equal, a fly with this
> gene is more likely to have red eyes than a fly without
> the gene." However, he defends talking about genes
> "for" particular characteristics on the ground that it
> is "routine genetic practice." And so it is.[1]

This is a good example of how our normal ways of speaking and our biases in thinking can keep us from accurately under-standing or describing a process. This business of a gene "for" blue eyes makes sense to us because it comes right out of the mechanism that informs our culture. That is, there is a gene "for" brown eyes just as there is a button for the hazard lights on my car. Press the button, the hazards turn on. Don't press it, they stay off. So if I pass on to my daughter a gene for brown eyes, she'll have brown eyes. If I don't pass it on in the DNA dance of fer-tilization, she won't have them. Mechanism makes things simple and easy to understand.

But mechanism isn't the only possibility. We've seen how quantum physics defies pure mechanism with its indeterminacy and non-local action. In the field of biology, Sheldrake proposes that the genetic process works a bit differently from the orthodox mechanistic determinism: "From the point of view of the hypothesis of formative causation, DNA, or rather a small part of it, is responsible for the coding for RNA and the sequences of amino acids in proteins, and these have an essential role in the functioning and development of the organism. But the forms of the cells, tissues, organs, and the organisms as a whole are shaped not by DNA but by morphic fields."[2] These biological fields exert an influence that shapes the organism, whether it's a colt who turns out to be all black, or a baby who is a second blue-eyed daughter. Moreover, the morphic fields are sensitive to species and differentiate between them by a process of tuning: "Developing organisms are tuned to similar past organisms, which act as morphic 'transmitters.' Their tuning depends on the presence of appropriate genes and proteins, and genetic inheritance helps to explain why they are tuned in to morphic fields of their own species: a frog's egg tunes in to frog rather than newt or goldfish or chicken fields because it is already a frog cell containing frog genes and proteins."[3] Tuning is the process by which one type of morphic field rather than another influences a developing organism, and the genes which code for proteins invoke this tuning. So the morphic fields and the genes work together. This "tuning" analogy is loosely reminiscent of how television sets are tuned to receive the pictures and sounds of NBC by virtue of the construction of the set and its internal parts, whereas radios are tuned to receive the latest pop hits on WZOO 100.3, because that is the way the radio is constructed. And just as there would be no prime-time sitcoms without the television set and the television waves working together, so there would be no sweet-natured blue-eyed daughter without the genes and morphic fields working together.

Sheldrake assumes that the morphogenetic or morphic fields

are real and interact closely with matter, just as gravitational fields and electromagnetic fields are real and interact with matter. He didn't originate the concept of form–producing fields, and mentions the earlier scientists who introduced and then explored the idea. What is new in his hypothesis of formative causation is the influence of the past. "The structure of these fields is not determined by either transcendent Ideas or timeless mathematical formulae, but rather results from the actual forms of previous similar organisms. Thus, for example, the morphogenetic fields of the foxglove species are shaped by influences from previously existing foxgloves. They represent a kind of pooled or collective memory of the species. Each member of the species is molded by these species fields, and in turn contributes to them, influencing future member of the species."[4] I could imagine that the fetus developing inside Loraygold has a certain genetic profile, and all things being equal, this genetic profile is more likely to produce a frisky Tobiano foal. This is the "what" happens. "How" it happens is that the morphic fields of past Tobiano foals would be attuned to this DNA through its similarity to past Tobiano foal DNA; those fields would reach through time and space to cooperate with it and to organize the development of the embryo so that it actually becomes a Tobiano foal. The specific morphic fields for a specific kind of colt would be triggered by the proteins coded for by the genes the colt has actually inherited. I do hope the foal is female, because gelding unnerves me. Besides, my new husband lives with me, my two daughters, his daughter part-time, the new daughter we are expecting, a female dog and female cat, and he might go to extraordinary lengths to preserve the structural integrity of the only other male member of the family.

The process by which morphogenetic fields reach through time and space is the process of morphic resonance, which acts through similarity. A developing Tobiano foal is subject to the accumulated morphic resonance of all the Tobiano foals that came before it, which is a kind of resonance through time. It's this resonance that sets the morphogenetic fields. Morphic resonance transfers information, but not energy. It "is a kind of action at a distance in both space and time. The hypothesis assumes that this influence does not decline with distance in space or in time."[5] This resembles the "spooky action at a distance" of quantum mechanics. However, morphic fields don't involve the typical kinds of action–at–a–distance that we're used to dealing with, such as the light of stars traveling through an immense expanse of space and thousands of years to reach us as we stand on a grassy field at night with a high–school sweetheart. Sheldrake acknowledges that morphic resonance doesn't correspond exactly to the familiar fields of quantum physics. It does, however, make use of fundamental vibrations, the fact that everything ceaselessly vibrates—that's why it's a resonance principle. And memory, which is inherent in morphic fields, is also contained within our view of starlight: "The light reaching us from distant galaxies embodies a memory of them as they were millions of light years ago, and light is still reaching us from stars that have long since died."[6] Because the stars are long gone, we're actually seeing only a memory of them. Memory and vibration are everywhere in nature.

So how does morphic resonance travel through space and time? What's its medium? Sheldrake offers the possibility of a "morphogenetic ether," or another dimension. But he suggests that "a more satisfactory approach may be to think of the past as pressed up, as it were, against the present, and as potentially present everywhere."[7] It's possible that the "morphic ether" itself is what is pressed up against, or intertwined into the present, and so exists everywhere. Those two latter possibilities for how morphic resonance travels aren't mutually exclusive—and this is reminiscent of the spiritual ether that mystics characterize as being present everywhere.

In that morphic fields transmit information from the past, they are a kind of memory, and they evolve along with the systems they organize. They aren't fixed and static, but are dynamic. They're probabilistic, subject to indeterminism, for several reasons: no two systems with the same genetic make–up ever develop identically; morphic fields arise from the morphic resonance from countless previous similar systems, and no two are ever exactly the same, just like no two daisies or snowflakes are exactly the same; and morphic fields are, in all likelihood, "akin to quantum matter fields . . . The relationship of morphic fields to quantum matter fields is, of course, still obscure . . . These fields interact . . . if they are similar in kind to quantum matter fields, not only would their interactions be easier to conceive, but it would be possible to look forward to the development of a unified theory that would embrace both."[8] This is the holy grail of physics, after all—a unified theory—and morphic fields would integrate nicely, and thus bring biology into deeper alignment with our understanding of physics and with our spiritual sense of the unity of all things in a great field of intelligence.

Because morphic fields transmit information, Sheldrake claims that they can explain open questions in biology, such as that of acquired traits. These are physical traits that develop under unusual situations, such as exposing fruit fly embryos to certain gases like ether, which makes some of them develop, for example, abnormal wings. The abnormal wings then recur in future generations of fruit flies whose embryos have not been exposed to ether. Another example of acquired traits are traits that seem to develop because of habitual use, such as the way camels have knee pads to protect their legs while kneeling. Baby camels are born with these knee pads. There has been some debate among biologists as to whether, in the case of the camels, the knee pads were acquired as a result of a habit of kneeling, and over countless generations became hereditary, and thus developed even in camel embryos before they'd ever kneeled. This is not a strictly mechanistic theory, and it contrasts with the theory that knee pads became inbred because of chance mutations which produced calluses in the right places, and were thus favored by natural selection. Either way, morphic fields offer another alternative. According to Sheldrake, "acquired characteristics can be inherited not because the genes are modified, but because this inheritance depends on morphic resonance."[9] The past comes into play when the morphic fields are tuned, and the fields themselves carry the information. They picked up the memory of the knee pads from the first camels who grew them, and then, carrying the information about knee pads, the fields attuned to camel embryos through morphic resonance, and, with accumulating strength, influenced the embryos to grow knee pads.

Sheldrake also questions the traditional theory of dominant and recessive genes, because dominance evolves. He points out that orthodox textbook explanations of dominance and recessive are speculative and untestable. We can't design a repeatable experiment which will clearly prove genetic dominance in action. Instead, he favors a dominance arrived at by morphic fields. That is, dominant characteristics, which we know evolve, grow stronger by virtue of having arisen from larger numbers of past organisms. They carry more weight of influence because they've been tuned to more frequently. Natural selection does play a role in this process, because if it favors a mutation, more and more organisms will be born with that mutation, which will make the morphic field stronger, more stable, and even more likely to influence future generations.

So there are alternatives to the pure mechanism of the physicochemical processes of genetics in biology. Sheldrake goes so far as to call these processes "over-rated." He insists that these mechanistic processes address the question of "what happens" but not of "how" and "why." But he doesn't discount genes, he simply reformulates their sphere of activity. He also adds in the action of morphic fields which act through time, and because of morphic fields, he argues for the possibility of acquired characteristics:

> **The phenomenon of heredity . . . depends both on genes and on morphic fields. The form and behavior of organisms are not coded or programmed in the genes any more than the TV programs picked up by a TV set are coded or programmed in its transistors. From the point of view of the hypothesis of formative causation, the orthodox genetic theory of inheritance involves a projection of the properties of morphic fields onto genes, an attempt to squeeze them into the molecules of DNA. Thus there are thought to be genes rather than morphic fields for particular structures and for patterns of behavior. Genes, rather than morphic fields, are assumed to be dominant or recessive; and the evolution of dominance is believed to depend on ill-defined genetic changes, rather than on the cumulative building up of habits by morphic resonance from large numbers of similar organisms in the past. The possibility of the inheritance of acquired characteristics is denied on theoretical grounds, just because it cannot be explained in terms of genes. But in fact it may happen because of morphic resonance. From this perspective, in the absence of morphic fields and morphic resonance, the role of genes is inevitably overrated, and properties are projected onto them that go far beyond their known chemical roles.[10]**

That is, we are so eager to put everything in mechanistic terms—we are so programmed by our culture that everything operates as machines do—that we credit genes and the genetic process with more power than they and it can possibly have. It's a sign of the infection of our culture by this mechanism. It shows how our thinking and articulating have taken the machine metaphor so literally that we are trapped inside it. As previously mentioned, the theory of morphic fields might also serve to reconcile the people who espouse the "intelligent design" theory of species development with those people who strictly support evolution. Human peace and progress depend not on rigid absolutism, but on richness and integration.

Sheldrake also credits morphic fields with shaping human and animal behavior, from the instinct of animals, to the learning of language or any kind of physical or mental skills by humans, to the formation of social and cultural organizations. This is all possible because of the memory aspect of morphic fields, memory referring to the information contained within the fields. It works simply, on the principles of attunement, organization, and hierarchy already described. Morphic fields attune to members of the same species, organize their characteristic or hereditary patterns of behavior in keeping with the patterns of behavior of past members of that species, and do so in hierarchical ways. That is, more complex, higher order patterns of behavior with more complex goals organize the less complex, lower order patterns of behavior with less complex goals. An example of this in human culture might be that the higher order, complex action of creating art, say a Michelangelo-esque standing nude figure, organizes the lower order, less complex behavior of shaping clay around an armature. Morphic fields thus explain why new patterns of behavior which are learned are then learned more quickly and easily by other members of the breed.

There is a famous, probably apocryphal story which seems to illustrate the actions of morphic fields. The story has been lauded by some and roundly denounced as a myth by others, but it serves, if nothing else, as a kind of allegory. It's called the "Hundredth Monkey Phenomenon," and was first told by Lyall Watson in his book *Lifetide* and then retold by Ken Keyes Jr. in *The Hundredth Monkey*. The story goes that the Japanese monkey, macaca fuscata, was observed in the wild for a number of decades. In 1952, on the island of Koshima, scientists were giving the monkeys sweet potatoes dropped in sand. The monkeys liked the sweet potatoes but not the dirty, gritty taste of the sand. A young female discovered that she could wash away the unpalatable sand in a nearby stream, though that was not a native habit of these monkeys. She then taught this trick to her mother and playmates. The other young monkeys taught their mothers. Over a number of years, as the scientists observed the monkeys, this "cultural innovation" was gradually picked up by other monkeys. Mostly it was young monkeys and their mothers who washed the potatoes, and the offspring of the younger monkeys. At a certain point, a certain critical number of monkeys—say ninety-nine of them—learned to do this, and suddenly, with the one–hundredth monkey learning to do so, the entire tribe of monkeys was washing the sand off the sweet potatoes. Thereafter, colonies of monkeys on nearby islands were also observed washing their sweet potatoes. This behavior had been spread to distant monkeys by the morphic field of the species. The learned behavior was held in the memory of the morphic field until enough monkeys had contributed to the strength of the field that the memory permeated the collective.

It may not be exactly true as told, but this story shows how morphic fields organize patterns of behavior, not just patterns of form. That is, morphic fields don't just give monkeys two hands with opposable thumbs, feet that look like hands, and prehensile tails that grip tree branches for swinging. Morphic fields also shape their behavior, both learned and innate or instinctual. Sheldrake relates similar stories, such as one about a young hunting dog who had never heard the sound of a gun, but when the gun went off, the dog started to search for a downed bird. Since the dog had never heard a gun shot before, nor been trained to act this way, this kind of behavior must be held in the morphic field of this breed of hunting dog. Enough past dogs had been trained to look for fallen birds when a shot was fired that the morphic field contained this behavior and had accumulated enough strength to influence the young dog in the present. Thus the young dog reacted spontaneously with this trained behavior, because it was attuned to the morphic field of its predecessors. These kinds of stories have been around for years, and Sheldrake relates "Charles Darwin himself took a great interest in such stories, and published an account in *Nature* of a mastiff's violent antipathy to butchers and butchers' shops, presumed to be due to mistreatment at the hands of a butcher, which was apparently transmitted to at least two generations of its offspring."[11]

Sheldrake doesn't just invoke Darwin himself in examining the role morphic fields play in instinct and learned behavior, he also describes experiments done on acquired memory and learned behavior. The famed Pavlov was said to have trained white mice to run to a particular feeding place when a bell was rung—he certainly made good use of bells, between this experiment and the celebrated one on conditioned salivation—and found that each subsequent generation of white mice learned this behavior faster and faster: "The first generation required an average of 300 trials to learn, the second only 100, the third 30, and the fourth 10."[12] Such results seem to have been too much for Pavlov, because he wasn't able to write conclusively on the topic of acquired memory, but left it open. Many scientists seem to react this way when evidence contradicts the pure determinism of the clockwork universe: It can't be so, so it isn't, and must be considered inconclusive. Another researcher named William McDougall performed experiments for over thirty years in Scotland and Australia. He set up an experiment with lab rats exiting a maze by either a lit exit in which they received an electric shock or a dim exit, where they didn't. McDougall discovered that each generation learned more quickly to take the safe exit. The first generation averaged over 165 errors, while the thirtieth generation averaged only 20. "McDougall showed that this striking improvement was not due to genetic selection for more intelligent rats, because even if he selected the most stupid rats in each generation as parents of the next, there was still a progressive increase in the rate of learning."[13] This experiment is readily explicable in terms of morphic fields which contain information and which accumulate strength over time with numbers of rats learning the correct exit. Naturally, mechanistic biologists didn't like McDougall's results, and they repeated his experiments. Oddly enough, the rats seemed to continue in the same vein, starting where McDougall's thirtieth generation had ended. This result lends further support to the theory of morphic fields. The memory had been established and stabilized within the morphic fields, and so another thirty generations weren't required to arrive at the same place. The past was present to these lab rats.

It all comes back to memory, and seeing memory as a field of influence that is not confined to chemical signatures within individual brains. Rather, fields of influence contain information and reach through time to affect similar organisms in the present:

> From a mechanistic point of view, memory depends on memory traces, as yet unidentified, which function in a manner that remains obscure . . . By contrast, according to formative causation, behavior is organized by morphic fields associated with the activities of the nervous system. The inheritance of instincts and the building up of an animal's own habits both depend on morphic resonance . . . For this reason, habits acquired by some animals can facilitate the acquisition of the same habits by other, similar animals, even in the absence of any known means of connection or communication.[14]

Morphic fields thus provide an explanation for instinctive behavior within a species. They also explain how individuals within the species develop their personal habits, such as how an individual dog can know to look for a fallen bird when it hears a gun fired, and how subsequent generations of a species can

learn an activity faster than previous ones. Those later generations, of course, have the benefit of the information accumulated
in the morphic fields over time.

Morphic fields operate similarly for human beings. Just as
animals are, we are influenced by the biological morphic fields
and by the behavioral morphic fields, which all contain memory.
So when we embark on the adventure of learning a new skill, we
learn things directly from more skilled or knowledgeable people,
but the morphic fields lend aid as well. There's a big field of
memory and information about how to do the skill present because of all the people who've done it in the past. So, in the
example of learning to hit a golf ball or to ride a horse, we attune
ourselves to the morphic fields which hold the accumulated
golfing or equestrian knowledge of generations of previous golfers and riders, and we can learn faster and more easily than our
predecessors. The fields teach us indirectly while a teacher does
so directly. The information simply seeps into our intelligence. I
think this is clearly visible in our own lifetime with computer
literacy. I labored in my twenties to figure out how to get a computer to do what I wished, while my children seemed to pick it
up quickly and effortlessly, as if by osmosis. I always ask my
oldest daughter first when I have a computer problem. At this
rate, my daughters' children will be born knowing how to program!

I wish I could say that I had demonstrated this principle of
morphic field memory in my own life, with horseback riding in
particular. I never cared that my golf swings inevitably went wild
and that I could only count on hitting other golfers, sand traps,
and water hazards, rather than the green. But I do want to ride
well. There have been enough generations of equestrians that the
morphic field must have accumulated quite a lot of strength.
However, it took me a very long time to learn to post with any
proficiency, and my cantering skills still leave something to be
desired. I'm determined because I like the warm, earthy feeling

of sitting astride a horse, and my heart thrills when I walk into a barn and inhale the perfume of fresh hay and fat barn cats and oiled leather tack and sweaty horses and horse defecation, but learning to ride hasn't been a quick or easy process. Again, as with computers, my slow learning contrasts with my daughters' rapid learning. Those two took to horseback riding as if they'd been born in a saddle. Do morphic fields influence the young more strongly than the old? Is it that the young have easier access to the information contained in morphic fields, because they're still forming, still developing organically? I wonder. Perhaps that's why regeneration is more available to young organisms, as well.

Notwithstanding my equestrian ineptitude, Sheldrake explores evidence of the influence of morphic fields from experiments and observations involving language learning, the rise in IQ levels, and tests with Morse code. He also recounts the results of an experiment sponsored by the Tarrytown Group of New York to test the hypothesis of formative causation. The group, with the British magazine *New Scientist*, held a competition for the best experiment, and a test involving unknown nursery rhymes in a foreign language won the competition. Sheldrake used Japanese rhymes, and was helped by a Japanese poet, who provided three rhymes: one a real nursery rhyme chanted by generations of Japanese children, one a fake rhyme that resembled the traditional rhyme but was new, and one a nonsense rhyme. It seemed reasonable that if the theory of morphic resonance holds true, the real rhyme, supported by its morphic resonance of having been learned by generations of Japanese children, would be much easier to learn than the fake rhyme and the nonsense rhyme. Sheldrake reports the results:

> **In a series of experiments with groups in Britain and America who learned the rhymes by chanting each of them a fixed number of times (without knowing which**

> was which), 62% of those tested found the genuine rhyme easiest to recall a half hour later. This result is far above chance expectation: if the rhymes were of equal difficulty, by chance about 33% of those tested would have been expected to recall the genuine rhyme better than they recalled the new ones . . . There were no consistent differences in the ease with which the two newly composed rhymes were learned.[15]

This experiment would seem to prove the existence of fields of information that influence learning, but Sheldrake cautions that the results, though encouraging, are not conclusive. More experiments need to be composed. He also mentions the possibilities which may arise from utilizing the principles of his theory of formative causation, should the weight of evidence favor it: Education might get easier and quicker. New methods of teaching that lead to improved learning would greatly enhance people's lives. Improving lives and opening minds are some of the highest goals of science, along with exploration and discovery, in which ways science resembles spirituality. Ultimately, science and spirituality are both about evolution and growth, and the enhancement of human life.

Sheldrake, courageously, was willing to frame old questions in new ways, and to grapple with unanswered questions and phenomena, in order to accommodate evolution and growth—and, hopefully, to stimulate some within the discipline of science itself. In his subsequent book *Seven Experiments that Could Change the World*, Sheldrake goes beyond morphic fields to examine curious, overlooked phenomena such as the reality of phantom limbs, the sense of being stared at, the extended mind, and the telepathy and prescience of pets. Everyone has experiences with these phenomena. Everyone knows the frisson on the back of the neck that's the tip-off to being stared at. And we all know stories of pets who know when their owner is coming home. Our cat Kitty Minky has a voluptuous, purring love for my new husband, and she skulks into the foyer a few minutes before he arrives home. It just consistently happens, and my husband is a sculptor whose hours are irregular. Whether he returns home at 8:00 p.m. or 6:00 p.m. depends on whether he's sculpting, which he will do for twelve hours a day, or he's telephoning galleries and collectors, organizing a show, shooting photos of the latest piece with a photographer, and engaging in marketing—in short, doing business, which he finds necessary but less pleasurable. The point is the cat always knows when to greet him. So we can all relate to these phenomena as real and truthful, and yet they've been brushed off by orthodox science. Orthodox science hasn't wanted to see the implications of these phenomena, which would shatter the grand machine and introduce soul, imagination, magic, and consciousness into the equation. Or perhaps a better way of expressing this would be to say that the grand machine would not be shattered, it would be transformed into a gelatinous structure with permeable, responsive boundaries, informed and operated by dynamic fields of influence, just as the human body/mind is. In this inclusive, alchemical way of thinking, the old Hermetic principle holds true: as above, so below; as within, so without. Mathematics and science are not separate from spirit and mysticism, but arise from it, and are seamlessly intertwined with it.

> There's a cosmic imagination, the imagination of the anima mundi, the soul of the universe. Within this are the imaginations of galaxies, solar systems, planets, ecosystems, societies, individual organisms, organs, tissues, and so on . . . The cosmic imagination seems to be engulfed within an eternal mathematical mind, when it may be no more mathematical than human beings are when we're dreaming . . . I'm suggesting that the cosmic imagination might include within it a mathematical realm, and that this mathematical realm is evolving just as our own understanding of mathematics is evolving in time.[16]

CHAPTER

5

The body is itself organized and pervaded by fields. As well as electromagnetic, gravitational, and quantum matter fields, morphogenetic fields shape its development and maintain its form. Behavioral, mental, and social fields underlie behavior and mental life. According to the hypothesis of formative causation, morphogenetic, behavioral, mental, and social fields are different kinds of morphic field, containing an inherent memory both from an individual's own past, and a collective memory from countless other people who have gone before . . . I am exploring the more general idea of fields as organizing patterns in space and time.[1]

The rigid mechanism of conventional science is failing rapidly, as we examine quantum physics and radical biological theories. Instead of being biological machines with minds localized inside the gray matter within our skulls, we are complex creatures, more like carbon–based, bilaterally symmetrical, bipedal nodes where many vibrations, forces, and fields intersect at a particular set of coordinates in space and time. Even those coordinates can't contain us. We stream out in all directions, in all dimensions, because the memory in morphic fields acts undiminished across space and time; because light, in the form of electromagnetic radiation, is also part of our being; and because the matter in our bodies is subject to quantum fields, which demonstrate bizarre, mind–bending principles like "reality is non–local." Even elementary physics tells us that every atom in our bodies was once a star that exploded. We are creatures of light, memory, probability, information: beings of consciousness. In some mysterious way that I think will make sense when physics finally achieves a Theory of Everything, light and consciousness are different states of the same essence, as water can be liquid, ice, or steam. One Cayce reading discussing the Akashic Records says, "Light moves on in time and space, and upon that skein between them the records are written by each soul in its activity through eternity. They are written through the soul's awareness, through its consciousness—not only in matter but in thought." (815–2) Consciousness affects light, time, space, and matter, which leads to a strange equivalency. Light and matter and consciousness are intermingled, and unified; light is consciousness is spirit; matter is condensed light and thus condensed thought; light, thought, consciousness is our very being. Cayce said, "What is light? That from which, through which, in which may be found all things, out of which all things come." (2533–8)

Growing up with moments of clairvoyance made me feel defective and uncomfortable, but I had the experience of literally seeing spiritual light, and I wouldn't trade that for anything. No matter how lonely and secretly alien I felt, I was still lucky to see that people live literally as seeds of light growing within a field of light. I shut down the seeing for ten years, in high school and college, and missed it as I would miss my four limbs or my liver. Opening it again when I started meditating in graduate school was a blessing and a relief. Because I was older and more experienced, I examined my perceptions more closely. I wanted to understand them and the phenomenon of clairvoyance more thoroughly. I read every book I could find on spirituality, the paranormal, and the psychic senses. I found the well-documented Cayce readings invaluable. I read modern mystics like Jane Roberts, Roslyn Bruyere, Alex Kardec, and Barbara Brennan. I sought out the work of scientists like Rupert Sheldrake and William Tiller who tried to actually explore psychic phenomena, as opposed to dismissing them on the thoroughly unscientific grounds that they can't exist, so they don't. I found inspiration in Sheldrake's willingness to examine unorthodox subjects like pet telepathy, the sense of being stared at, the reality of phantom limbs, and the extended mind. I took notice of my own thoughts and intentions when I perused physicist William Tiller's work on how subtle energies act on physical phenomena. My scrutiny took on more coherence when I went to spiritual healing school and acquired a vocabulary with which to reference my vision and a community of peers with whom to share it. It's hard, if not impossible, to make cogent observations about a phenomenon without a language that posits the phenomenon in the first place.

So what is this wonderful, mysterious, all-encompassing light of consciousness that mystics report, that many people think is inextricably related to the various fields that physics describes? What does it look like, how does it work? I don't have the final word by any means; my own vision and understanding are far too limited, idiosyncratic, and incomplete. I can only relate what I experience. To me, it looks a lot like diffuse pale sunlight. It's both universal and personal. I see it best when I'm in an expanded state, because of meditation or prayer. Once I spent a weekend at an ashram, chanting and meditating. Although I believe that the real challenge is to live a spiritual life as a house-holder in the world, not hidden away in a cave or ashram where it's easy to be blissful, I still occasionally go on retreats—and not just to take a much-needed break from kids, husband, pets, and work. I go to have a deeper, more palpable experience of the divine that is both immanent and transcendent in every moment.

On the occasion of my weekend at the ashram, I returned home in a powerfully exalted state. I stood on the street in Manhattan and saw myself surrounded by incomparable beauty: the grainy black pavement, the corner deli selling bundles of pink carnations, yellow taxis screeching and buses lumbering down the avenue, nannies pushing strollers and old men smoking cigars and people walking dogs or shopping or hawking books, all of them with the grace of God pouring out of their faces. In that moment the light was a golden fabric into which everything was woven. I stood still thanking God for the moment that I had lived to reach.

Usually I am not so expanded. Bustling my daughters off to school with all their homework, arranging with the stable up-state for Loraygold and Garfield to be shod, and sucking ginger candies to quell my morning sickness (or drinking limeade, which Cayce recommends and which definitely helps) don't loft me into celestial perception. In daily life, I catch a glimmer of mists and webs around people but I don't see the universal field. It's only when I am most open and grounded and lifted that I see more, and then the universal field looks to me like a soft golden luminescence that surrounds and interpenetrates everything—much like the "force" of *Star Wars* fame. Sometimes it looks like a vast, diaphanous river of gold pouring down from the sky. Floating within that river, like bubbles in a pond, is the individualized bubble around the kernel of the self. That bubble is the personal aura.

The greater field of light appears to hold the pattern for both macrocosm and microcosm. Every species and every creature, the evolution of universe and galaxy and planet and creature, every symphony and every poem or painting, is held as in idea in this unlimited field. It orders everything. There's something impersonal about it, though a first-hand experience of it is deeply intimate. This observation relates directly to the morphic fields, which contain the same information, and are also both impersonal and intimate. After all, the morphic field that holds the template for a developing fetus has accumulated its influence from countless generations of human beings, and it operates through a natural process of morphic resonance, so it is impersonal in that sense. However, when a specific fetus being influenced by morphic fields is developing inside my womb, and will emerge in a few weeks as a new daughter we plan to name Madeleine, that's intimacy.

In contrast, the aura is personal. Everything we are, everything we do, is described in our aura. Cayce says that,

> **Auras are twofold: that which indicates the physical emanations, and that which indicates spiritual development. These, when they are kept more in accord with the experience of the individuals, make for greater unification of purpose and ideal. The aura, then, is the emanation that arises from the very vibratory influences of an individual, mentally and spiritually—especially from the spiritual forces.**
> **319-2**

Again the idea of vibration and emanation occur, showing how fundamental vibration, resonance, and radiation are to the workings of all things, a matter on which science and mysticism agree.

Artists have painted the spirit bodies that embrace the physical one, clairvoyants have seen them, poets have described them, and the literature of spirituality richly depicts them. The nature of the aura is still often mysterious. Cayce sometimes describes it as "clothing" or "cloaking" the body, but he also says that the aura controls the body: "All bodies radiate those vibrations with which it, the body, controls itself in mental, in physical, and such radiation is called the aura." (5756-1) I'm convinced that even the word "radiate" fails to capture the true extent, the true meaning of the aura, that personal, individuated light within the greater ocean of light that is universal consciousness. The aura is more than a pretty refraction thrown by the soul. It is literally our being. It contains us. Watching auras has led me to believe that light and consciousness engender the flesh. We are in fact creatures of light streaming into bodies in the material world. Our origins lie in those spiritual realms that are spaceless and timeless; we pierce time and space in order to reach the unitive place that is our ground of being.

In the dimensionless place where time and space fall away, we find unity with the divine, with ourselves, and with other people. Differences, like all illusions, evaporate. That's what makes the notion of the mechanical universe so dangerous: it perpetuates illusions of separateness, of the unbreakable rigidity of time and space. We find ourselves hopeless and isolated inside an unresponsive cosmic box with immutable laws. And this mechanism has a firm grip on conventional science, which our culture reveres, despite Einstein telling us that time is not constant and quantum physics revealing that reality is non-local, probabilistic and indetermined. I think Cayce said it best when he claimed that "time and space are the elements of man's own concept of the infinite and are not realities." (2533-8) Physicist William Tiller, whose work we will examine in the next chapter, agrees: "As Emanual Kant said long ago, time and space are merely our vehicles for perception—they are not reality itself."[2]

So, in the most literal sense, people are multidimensional. We partake of non-local reality, quantum indeterminacy, and the elasticity of time—which pertain to mysticism and spirit, not just hard science. Our many dimensions are thus both material and spiritual. We inhabit physical realms, like Newton's mechanical frame of reference, Einstein's smooth geometric cosmos, and the quantum universe's raucous field of probability, and celestial realms, like the ether which contains the Akashic Records. It's not necessary to be a clairvoyant like Edgar Cayce to experience this with vibrant immediacy. Prayer and meditation reveal fundamental truths to sincere seekers. We are greater than we imagine as we go about our day, driving our children to school, scrubbing oatmeal out of the breakfast bowls, meeting with clients in a woody conference room. It's imperative that we find the science that describes our multidimensionality, because one key to transforming our society and bettering the world is uniting spirit with science.

This process of transformation begins at the grass roots level, within the individual. We each start with our own lives and move outward from there. The Cayce readings state, " . . . the simplicity of individuals to apply that as may be obtained from their own subconscious self, cosmic forces and universal consciousness (or call it by whatever name the individual may choose)—this is the great truth that must be apparent to the layman, the individual, the scientist, the mathematician, the historian." (254–46) This speaks to the importance of each individual turning within, to self-examination and personal experience of the Divine. We need to experience for ourselves, directly and tangibly, that we are beings of light who focus fields of consciousness. This personal experience is crucial; it's the impetus toward transformation. I certainly wouldn't have gone looking for the mystical action of spirit if it hadn't grabbed me by the collar and shaken me first. So we begin by exploring our own consciousness and searching ourselves for light. Uncovering the light within isn't a one–time only, miraculous act of redemption, atonement, or communion with God. It's an ongoing process of self-examination. Patience and commitment to the process are what matter, not clairvoyance or impressive psychic abilities. Cayce spoke of the importance of patience as we wind our way through the plastic constructs of time and space in this process: "Yet out of Time, Space, Patience, is it possible for the consciousness of the finite to *know* the infinite." (262–115)

In this way, we are all transformers, because the process is accessible to each of us. It begins the first time we swing the arc of perception within to witness our own inner workings. A neutral curiosity emerges: What is here, now? Why?

My experience is that these questions deepen over time, rather than acquire answers. I admit that I frequently don't enjoy the process. When I apply myself honestly to the questions, "What is here, now? Why?" I usually end up squirming. I find that what is here, now, is the little Navy brat kid with long brown braids and too–big eyes who sees the world in turmoil, flux, and constant change. She barely trusts anyone. She's terrified, deeply rebellious, and has a hard time walking away from a fight. This little girl isn't my only or better self, I hope, but I can own her existence. I can even respect her place within me. By doing so, I integrate her with the other parts of me that aren't so distrusting, ferocious, and scared. Because it is also she who reaches out to the divine, who lets herself see figures of light, who opens to spontaneous joy, and who bubbles with creativity. She's worth including in my psyche. When I agree to understand her, she opens the door to understanding how other people can be different from me, harboring traits I don't understand or perhaps admire, and yet those people are also like me. It's alchemical. The shadow that I own becomes the light that I have to share.

Self–examination, meditation, and prayer, taken together, are a journey into greater and greater consciousness. The journey has been much discussed in the Cayce readings and well chronicled in metaphysical tracts like the Upanishads, the Tibetan Book of the Dead, and the Kabbalah. Along the path are certain land-marks that every individual undertaking the journey passes, in some order personally meaningful to him or her: intuition, clair-voyance, synchronicity, precognition, telepathy, reincarnation, telekinesis, transfiguration, transcendence. These are some of the signposts along the way that indicate something—not progress, but rather commitment. Any sincere seeker eventually has expe-riences that shatter normal definitions of reality; it's about time that scientists like Sheldrake and Tiller began to examine these experiences as if they mattered. Sometimes there's simply a grow-ing certainty that there is more, that the divine is immanent and transcendent in every moment, every cell, every particle, every angstrom of light. Whatever form those experiences take, they lead to an inescapable conclusion: the mundane physical world is only camouflage for the greater spiritual reality in which we have our being.

Because we originate in a greater reality that is outside of time and space, this lifetime imposes only a tenuous and permeable boundary around each of us. It follows that this lifetime doesn't define us. It isn't our only one. I can't write a book called *Piercing Time and Space* that focuses on Edgar Cayce without mentioning reincarnation. In his psychic readings, Cayce offered details of many past lives. In the beginning, the concept of reincarnation troubled the plain–spoken and devoted Christian man. He went back to the Bible, which he had read cover to cover countless times, and found enough to sustain him in verses like "In my father's house are many mansions." (John 14:2) When he had resolved the crisis in his mind, Cayce began to add "life readings" to the physical readings he gave. Life readings included in-formation about past lives and were given for the purpose of helping people evolve and progress: "Hence, in man's analysis and understanding of himself, it is as well to know from whence he came as to know whither he is going." (5753-1) Memory of the past helps shape evolution and offers options to consciousness.

Cayce's life readings were detailed and specific: "Before this the entity was among those peoples to whom the inventor of the steam's application to the motor, or in France, to whom Fulton went—in the name of Eben Claire, and the entity . . . aided in the material surroundings, but during the sojourn in that experience applied self in attempting to determine ways and means and manners that were gathered by the entity Eben in its association with that body Fulton." (490-1) Details weren't given for fun and curiosity, but to show something important that was learned: "Little has been heard . . . of the entity's activities in that sojourn along the Seine, yet much in the soul development, much in the abilities of the entity in the present in *determination* arises from the experiences in that particular period." ((490-1) Cayce's psychic source read lifetimes spanning earth's history: "the entity in the name Guiraleldio, was that one who aided DaVinci," (490-1) "Before that we find the entity was in what is now known as the Egyptian period just previous to the incoming of that ruler from the Caucasian and Persian lands." (833-1) "Before that the entity was in the Roman land, during those periods just following the sojourn of Him who is the way, the truth and the light in the earth. The entity was a companion of one who was an emissary, or a teacher, or a lawmaker . . . in the name of Cassius, and the companion or wife of one Claudius—a follower of that procurator who sentenced the Master." (2144-1) Cayce's source read the Akashic Records and the information contained in other subconscious minds to get this information about past lives, information which was to be used for purposes of growth, development, and the soul's evolution.

Those other lifetimes affect us, sometimes profoundly. In turn,

paradoxically, we affect those other lifetimes. In fact, many para-
doxes open up when examining reincarnation and consciousness. Two in particular have to do with time. The first is that this
life is unspeakably precious, and yet it has been preceded by
many other precious lifetimes. Because time is not a static and
linear phenomenon, future lifetimes also present. This brings up
the second paradox: that all of time is happening at once, so the
notion of lifetimes is just a metaphor, anyway. They aren't really
happening in linear fashion, like gleaming pearls following one
another on a silken string that we can examine through a glass
darkly. What we do in each moment affects every past life and
future life, because time, like consciousness, is ultimately an
unbroken whole. We change our past and our future when
we transform ourselves in this moment—which is why Cayce
spoke of the Akashic Records as "old and ever new." (2144-1)
   We're always revising our history, always recreating ourselves
and our possibilities. Seeing time this way is a powerful part of
that process of understanding ourselves. Time, like space, is non-
local.
   I always knew I had lived other lives, without articulating it to
myself in this language, which I did not know as a girl. I simply
grew up with additional memories. They were sketchy but distinct, and they packed the same emotional wallop that the memories of this lifetime do. Some memories revolved around living in
a great house as the beloved wife of a wealthy man. When I was
a kid vacuuming the carpet or folding the laundry, I used to
mutter to myself about how nice having servants used to be. It
gave me something of an obnoxious Marie Antoinette complex,
much to my family's chagrin. It can't have been fun to have a
daughter or sister with the attitude that she was really an aris-
tocrat. But the memories of that lifetime stopped abruptly, and I
had a vague sense of having died prematurely.
   In the way that synchronicity works, I got to see the mansion

in which I had lived that cosseted life. It still stands, a great house on a river, offering tours. One summery Saturday afternoon when I was eleven, my parents, who were not sightseers, took my sister and me on a rare excursion to visit it. The night before, I dreamt about the house in detail. When I finally walked up the gray stone steps leading to the porch, chills crawled down my spine. Gooseflesh broke out all over my body. I knew this place. I had been here before. More than that—I had belonged here. I was home. We took a tour with a guide but I knew more about the house than she did. Tumultuous feelings flooded through me: sadness, longing, jealousy when I saw that some small thing had changed after I had left, after I had died. A poignant sense of sweetness settled in as I stood on the porch and stared across the rolling green lawn at the river. I had been loved here, love was real, and love would find me again. Not in the same form, but the truth of love was undeniable.

The memories from that lifetime weren't orderly and sequential as in reels from a movie. They were scattered through emotion-laden fragments, some larger than others. I have never recovered a complete narrative, and I seldom think of that life. It just doesn't pertain to my daily activities. This is where being grounded and centered is helpful. It keeps common sense in play. Do I really need to revisit the years as an ascetic in a medieval monastery while I'm painting faces at a carnival in my daughter's school? It isn't practicable, and besides, I keep learning with ever greater clarity that the most important moment is now, the most important lifetime this one, the most important spiritual awareness isn't of past lives but of the process of staying present in this life with my own feelings, assumptions, and projections. It is another paradox that as I grow more current, my past life memories get clearer. They are more accessible but less imposing. I am freed to live my everyday life as a wholer person. Wholeness is the prize here; it's what happens when all the parts are integrated, when time and space are breached by awareness, when mechanistic determinism is animated by something greater than mathematical principles: consciousness.

CHAPTER

6

One of the central, defining events of my life is the divorce from my first husband. It wasn't a single day's happening, but took place over a three-and-a-half-year period, much of which was heartbreaking, excruciating, soul-crushing—and those were its high points. Still, if it wasn't unified in time and space, this period is a Rubicon that divides my life irrevocably into a "before" and an "after." Before the divorce, I thought of myself and my life in a certain way, and I cultivated certain intentions; after it, I thought and intended differently. Because of the impact that thoughts and intention make on reality, my whole experience of reality has shifted.

I was seventeen when I met my former husband. He was different from anyone I'd ever met, full of expectations and assumptions of life that his wealthy, well-educated, East Coast Jewish family had programmed into him, expectations and assumptions that were completely alien to what had been programmed into me, as the daughter of an enlisted man in the Navy, from a farm and factory–working family spread out in the Midwest and South. My mother was a high school drop–out, my grandmother an itinerant farm worker with a third–grade education, and I was, in fact, the first person in my family to attend college. I can't take credit for the decision to go; my genius high school boyfriend with the nifty telescope had informed me matter–of–factly that I should. So much of the quality of our lives depends on the people we meet, and I owe this man a debt of gratitude for bettering my life. Based on my good grades, my old boyfriend had suggestions as to where I should apply. It hadn't occurred to me that college was even an option for someone from my background, but it seemed like a better idea than marrying a sailor, which was what my mother had done at the same age. Besides, it would be a splendid adventure to go off to learn new things. I followed his advice and filled out applications.

My ex–husband, who hailed from the next town over, tele-phoned me out of the blue the summer before my freshman year. "I'm assigned to be your Big Brother and show you around campus," he said, introducing himself. "Why don't I come over and we'll meet?" I agreed and went to inform my mother.

"I read about his family in the newspaper," she said, puffing on her ubiquitous cigarette. Indeed, his parents are pillars of the community, donating generously of time and money to civic causes, scholarship funds, and local museums. His aunt was in-volved in local politics and had, to her credit, made a difference. Thoughtfully my mother let scrims of smoke fill her eyes. She said, "They're Jews. If he comes for dinner, we can't serve pork chops."

"Or bacon cheeseburgers," I agreed. Uneasily we discussed ways of speaking and acting that might discomfit him. We'd never before hosted a Jew in our home, and we wanted to do it right, with grace and respect for him. We wanted him to feel comfortable.

We needn't have worried. My former husband, with a humor and zest I came to cherish as typically his, made himself right at home. He leapt at the offer of a burger, asking if there was cheese and bacon to top it. At his request, my mother, who is exotic and high cheekboned with the look of her Cherokee ancestors, gave me a sloe-eyed look. I shrugged, and he tore into the non-kosher meal with relish.

A sizzle sparked up between us after my freshman year, and he told me on our first date—to a drive-in feature of *The Groove Tube* and *Flesh Gordon*—that, if we got serious, I would have to convert to Judaism. "No problem," I shrugged. It seemed obvious that God and religion are separate entities, that God was everything and religion was just a convenient formal structure for worship. I didn't understand, at the time, that God and religion were the least of the issues. I could embrace the love of Torah and the rules of kashrut; I could light Shabbat candles with tenderness and gratitude to the Creator; and I could even pick up a smattering of Hebrew to follow services in synagogue; but I could never be culturally similar to my former husband. It's not in my hard-wiring; I eluded the morphic fields that carry those patterns of behavior. So no matter how deeply I loved him, and he loved me, ultimately I could not thrive in the context of his extended family's values or their "keep it in the family, keep it in the tribe" way of life. For him, it was a safe, closely-knit, secure structure, a strong base from which to live in the world; for me, it was closed, claustrophobic, suffocating, and creativity killing. I felt that his family siphoned off my individuality. He felt that I was anti-social. I felt like I was living in the Borg collective of *Star Trek: The Next Generation* fame. He thought I was crazy.

These fundamental cultural differences widened into a chasm between us, and led us each to devalue the other and to polarize

ever more cruelly. I thought of him as married to his family instead of to me, as boxed in by their xenophobic values, as rigid
and controlling. He thought of me as difficult, demanding, and
dependent. His conception of me, and what he wanted me to be,
also influenced the way I thought of myself: as a housewife and
mother who could never achieve lift–off in her career, who didn't
earn much money and who couldn't survive in the world without him. I didn't like this image of myself, but it filled me. I was
committed to the marriage, and I couldn't figure out how to
change the underlying images and continue in the marriage.

We had personal differences, too, that exacerbated matters. My
ex–husband is a brilliant and driven businessman who works
relentlessly a hundred hours a week. He's smart, successful, good
at negotiating with, and handling, people, which he does all day
long. He wants to relax and watch sports when he returns home—
basketball, football, baseball, golf, soccer, hockey, volleyball, professional or college; if nothing else is on, extreme bowling. I'm a
cantankerous writer and a dedicated mother, and after closeting
myself alone with my computer all day until the girls come back
from school, and then overseeing their homework and extracur-
ricular activities, I want to go outside and play. I want to run, do
yoga, ride bikes in the park, or, heaven forbid, saddle up an
opinionated horse. Why watch sports on TV when you can go do
them in real life? I want to talk about auras and the cosmos,
about "aurochs and angels, the secret of durable pigments, prophetic sonnets, the refuge of art."[1] He wanted to discuss his latest
deal, real estate prices, stocks and bonds, politics, last night's
Knicks game, and Tiger Woods. He has an incisive, ironic intelligence and conversation with him was never boring. It just didn't
reach me where I live.

Our deepest divergence is that I have a conviction that life is
a grand adventure to be passionately lived for learning and exploration. I want to show up with a thousand percent of myself

and intensely engage in every moment of this life; I enjoy trying new activities and grappling with new ideas; that's why I went to college when no one in my family had ever done so. I'm willing to break bounds, look stupid, and screw up in the pursuit of something more. More "what" I haven't precisely defined, but it has something to do with fulfillment and discovery. Adventure was not the top priority for my former husband's family. Millennia of persecution, including pogroms, the diaspora, and the loss of family members during the Holocaust, had made adventure seem frivolous and beside the point. My ex-husband went to college because that's what people in his family do: go to a good college and find a stable, moneymaking profession. There's nothing wrong with his way of life, and it's an excellent way to raise children. It just didn't suit me. It left me feeling empty. There's also nothing wrong with my needs or my approach to life, either, though he was always quick to mock them. It made me angry and defensive, and my worst self, all one thousand percent of her, pounced out into the ring, yelling and fighting, to confront my former husband. In retrospect, I can see that our cultural and individual differences, instead of enriching our lives, cascaded into a failure of love: My adult self couldn't give enough love to him, and my child self couldn't receive enough love from him. And vice-versa.

And perhaps we weren't equipped to appreciate each other appropriately. In comparing my first marriage with this second one, it's been a lesson to me on the power of perception and projection. How we frame an issue determines everything: "Mind is the builder," as the Cayce readings insist. If the mind perceives something as positive, or as negative, then it is. For example, my ex-husband often said, "You're so relentless! You're like the Terminator!" It was one of those pejorative catch-phrases that people in bad relationships latch onto, and it did nothing to shore up my self-esteem. In all fairness, I can't blame my ex-husband for the way he framed my personality. If I was on the receiving end of one of my ferocious harangues about picking up dirty socks, I'd probably think I was the Terminator, too.

In contrast, my new husband has a different perspective on me. One day as we walked down the street together before we were married, I said something in my typically emphatic fashion to my then–boyfriend. He broke into laughter. He reached over and hugged me. "You're so determined! You're like Wonder Woman!" he said. To this day, he calls me "Wonder Woman" and leaves sticky notes on my computer screen addressed to "Wonder Woman." Both men alluded to the same quality of tenacity that's part of my character. However, each experienced it differently. Each responded to it differently. For me, it feels better to be referred to as "Wonder Woman" than as "The Terminator," and I mean no disrespect to Governor Schwarzenegger.

Being thought of a certain way makes more than a superficial impact. It's not a simple matter of narcissism. We're all interwoven in the great field of consciousness, and other people's opinions of us carry weight, influence our self–image, and so shape our destiny, most profoundly so in intimate relationships. My new husband always thought of me as competent, capable, intelligent, and as a successful writer, which I longed to be. He didn't see me as needing anyone to survive. He's an artist himself and well understands the process of developing skill and honing craft, sending work out into the world and receiving rejection, and patiently persevering through to success. He also has great tolerance for the passionate artistic temperament, so he shrugs off my mercurial and contrary nature, and my rampages of both love and anger. We don't have a perfect relationship by any means, and there's a huge financial insecurity besetting us, but his supportive vision helped transform the way I thought of myself. That changed what I experienced in the world. The day my ex–husband moved out, I received the first acceptance for

publication of a poem. From then on, my poems and short stories began to be published. It's been a slow process and taken a
lot of hard work, but my career has begun to happen. Recently
I even started to earn money as a writer. Slowly I began to think
of myself not as the stay–at–home mom and housewife who
dabbled in writing of my first marriage, but as a hard–working,
income–earning mother who is producing a body of work in
which she can take pride.

More than my self–image and career shifted when my former
husband moved out, after seven years of dating and then thir-
teen years of marriage, twenty years of being a couple in total.
Between the two of us, things got ugly. Not at first; he still hoped
to resolve our problems and salvage the marriage. As it became
clear that the relationship had decayed beyond repair, and, I
guess, as he realized that he didn't want to reconcile because I
wasn't right for him, either, skirmishes broke out. We both felt
rejected and abandoned. We fought, with lawyers and without,
over the typical issues: money and children. We fought bitterly
because people do that when they still care for each other and
have to let go. It hurts to end a relationship, especially one that
began when both people were teenagers.

My former husband and I had done years of fruitless marriage
counseling, and now we each sought individual therapy. I eventually found a therapist who did spiritual work as well as talk
therapy. My therapist counseled me to meditate, pray, and practice yoga to work through my grief, despair, pain, and rage. He
also admonished me to monitor my thoughts about my ex–husband. Because we are all connected in the field of universal consciousness, my therapist explained, my thoughts about my former
mate were of utmost importance. They would reach him, resonate within him, and elicit a response in his consciousness, even
if he wasn't aware of it. I could perhaps influence the quality of
our interactions, because if I sent anger and hostility at him, he

would only respond in kind; whereas if I took the charge out of my view of him, there was a possibility for a cease–fire. Even if he didn't respond to my seeing him as a good man who was suffering, I would feel more peaceful. My mind and spirit would ease. I would reap the benefits of not harboring anger and nega–tivity, of not being consumed by the battle. I would have pre–ferred to send my daughters to salvage their father's toenail clippings, which he likes to leave out on the coffee table, and then have the girls bring the clippings home to me so I could perform voo–doo on him. I had luscious fantasies about a weird oozing rash stippling his body and a baby grand piano falling on his head in a thunderous arpeggio. But I was willing to try it my therapist's way.

And sometimes it works. There are times when I can hold onto my ex–husband's intelligence, humor, loyalty, and generosity, all the qualities that I admired about him when we were together, and the tensions between us seem to ease. Two years ago the man even paid to refurbish my kitchen with tile floors, granite countertops, and custom cherry cabinets. It was a breathtaking act of generosity, and though his daughters benefit from the new kitchen, he certainly didn't have to make such a grand gesture. There are other times when he berates me and threatens to take me to court, where he will have everyone I've ever met testify that I am crazy. On those occasions, I respond with every vicious thing I can think of to say—and because I'm a writer, I have oodles of nasty words at my disposal. Because I've known him for more than twenty years, I know which of those words will slink through the chinks in his armor. And I get off the phone with him and try to figure out how to hurt him back. Which is pretty much a fruitless indulgence on my part. Though I get furious, I can't sustain it, and the malice aforethought inevitably dissipates. What's left is the lingering low opinion of my former husband, which he doesn't really deserve, and the need to, once again, school my own thoughts about my former husband and restructure my own intentionality toward our relationship.

These are personal, relational examples of how, as physicist William Tiller puts it, "human intention acts like a typical potential capable of creating robust effects in what we call physical reality."[2] That is, my former husband and my current husband each have an intention toward me, and that intention has influenced my life. My former husband's intention toward me and mine toward myself seemed to cancel each other out, while my new husband's intention reinforces mine and results in dynamic growth for me. I also have intention toward these two men, and part of my work as someone on a spiritual journey, someone who wants to evolve toward her better self, is to be meticulous with regard to my intentionality—oozing rashes and crashing pianos notwithstanding.

Reading Tiller's work on science and consciousness underscores the urgency of being aware of my own intentionality. He has researched and documented the effects of intentionality, and proposed scientific reasons for its power. Dr. Tiller is a professor, researcher, author, and consultant. He's Professor Emeritus of the Department of Materials Science and Engineering at Stanford University. He's published over 250 scientific papers and three books, and he holds several patents. Currently he's something of a celebrity because of his erudite presence in the movie *What the #$BLEEP*! Do We Know?* In this charming and provocative film, he's the slim, gray–bearded gentleman with the twinkle in his eye, commenting thoughtfully on quantum physics and intentionality as he sits indoors next to his two books: *Science and Human Transformation* and *Conscious Acts of Creation*. Tiller has been seriously exploring the field of psycho–energetics and spiritual development for the past thirty years, and he's published an additional 100 scientific papers, as well as the two books, on this topic. In the first book, Tiller relates a personal example that parallels my experiences with my former and current husbands of what he calls a ""band broadening" effect":

> A personal example of this "band broadening" effect that had a profound impact on me occurred on several occasions when I was acting as a technical consultant to a certain U.S. company. An individual scientist would be describing his research and relating where he was blocked in his current project. I would be listening carefully, even when the technical area was not one where I was truly expert, and would be simultaneously radiating emotional support and encouragement to him. On these special occasions, it was as if I could tap his knowledge banks on the subject and suddenly his bandwidth, $^{TM}v_1$, and my bandwidth, $^{TM}v_2$, coupled to produce a resultant bandwidth of $^{TM}v_1 + {}^{TM}v_2$. Then, a cascade of new ideas relevant to his project would appear in my head. As we talked further, these ideas usually formed the vehicle for unblocking his project, allowing him to move forward with renewed confidence and vigor. For me, it was a joyfully creative outpouring and I basked in the flow knowing that it was unlikely to have occurred without the broader bandwidth of our cooperative mode being available for the information flow process.[3]

In this example, Tiller plays the supporting role, similar to the way my new husband "broadens the band" and supports me with a vision of myself as a successful author, and so helps me bring that about. Cayce might have said that my new husband's mind and my mind were building the image together, and so building that reality.

As can be seen in the quote above, Tiller comes out of a rigorous scientific background, complete with mathematical equations to describe the processes he is discussing. In *Science and Human Transformation*, he says frankly that "A new door has opened . . . a new adventure is afoot for science . . . we must find a valid larger perspective or new mindset which is needed to qualitatively describe this class of seemingly strange phenomena on an equal footing with our conventional scientific phenomena."[4] Like Sheldrake, Tiller takes seriously the unexplained phenomena that orthodox science would prefer to dismiss on the grounds that they can't exist, so they don't, or else there's some undiscovered but perfectly workable mechanistic explanation. Tiller begins by discussing the traditional mechanistic "formula" for living organisms, which he writes as:

$$\text{Function} \longleftrightarrow \text{Structure} \longleftrightarrow \text{Chemistry}^5$$

From this starting point, Tiller argues that electromagnetic fields must be included, because "as one digs deeper into the nature of living systems, one finds that they are very complex photoelectrochemical devices that emit a wide spectrum of photons, and that homeostasis at the chemical level requires a network of fields and currents flowing within the fabric of the body's cells and tissues."[6] In short, we are creatures of light—of electromagnetic fields—and that cannot be ignored. Tiller then discusses the mind–body connection, pointing to martial arts and yoga, which strengthen the link between mind, structure, and function; modern psychotherapy, which relies on the mutual influence of chemical states and mental states; acupuncture points on the human body, which demonstrate measurable electrical effects; and biofeedback, which can train the mind to direct temperature, blood flow, and electrical current to different parts of the body. Because of these phenomena, Tiller states, mind must be included in an expanded equation:

$$\text{Function} \longleftrightarrow \text{Structure} \longleftrightarrow \text{Chemistry} \longleftrightarrow \text{Electromagnetic Energy}$$
$$\text{Fields} \longleftrightarrow \text{Mind}^7$$

Sheldrake makes the same point in *The Presence of the Past*: "The nature of life and consciousness are not in practice taken into account in the actual theories of physics. These are the concerns of other departments. But if a truly unified theory is ever to emerge, living organisms and conscious minds must be included within it along with the particles and fields of physics. There is a need for a new natural philosophy that goes further than physics alone can go but remains in harmony with it."[8] The box of orthodox science must be dismantled—and restructured, perhaps as a hypercube.

In a practical, research–oriented way, Tiller discusses experiments to prove the validity of his revised equation. He mentions a device he himself designed, built, and tested with some of his students at Stanford, something he calls a "Biological Radiation Detector." This detector was able to register the measurable effects of self–directed mind, that is, intentionality. Tiller also writes about some psychokinesis studies and a study that monitored the energy emitted by a healer. These studies and his own experiments lead him to propose that "Mind should definitely be a term in [the] Equation but also that there is perhaps another unique energy form emitted by the body that should be located between mind and electromagnetic energy fields!"[9] Tiller calls that energy form "subtle energy fields," which are also known as the aura. He includes photographs that seem to show subtle energies around and between people. Bizarrely enough, some of these photographs were taken with the lens cap on the camera! He concludes that "subtle energies exist for which the camera lens cap and the human body are at least semi–transparent . . . Indeed, this expression of God's universe shows us that there are many more levels of manifestation in nature than our science has thus far uncovered."[10]

Because he is willing to state that subtle energies exist and therefore are to be examined, Tiller lists, in a straightforward fashion, what he calls "subtle energy phenomena." On his list are telepathy and precognition, which Sheldrake also presented as worthy of closer study (though Sheldrake, the biologist, is specifically interested in pet telepathy and prescience, and the human telepathic experience known as "the sense of being stared at.") Tiller includes remote viewing, auric sight/clairvoyance, clairaudience, psychometry, dowsing, healing/Qigong, psychokinesis/ telekinesis, dematerialization/materialization, levitation, and homeopathy. Regarding remote viewing, which is a strictly organized, thoroughly documented psychic protocol developed by the United States Army's STARGATE program during the Cold War, for the express purpose of spying,[11] Tiller notes that a "remote viewer may even perceive the scene before the target individual gets there. Thus, in general, the future time coordinate as well as the remote distance coordinate can be accessed by using a well–defined set of techniques, possibilities not allowed via the presently accepted paradigm."[12] In other words, a point in time, even in the future, is just as accessible to psychic remote viewing as a point in space; they're all just coordinate points. And governmental paranoia being what it is, it figures that if there is a way to pierce time and space for strategic advantage, the military would find and use it.

Given the gaps in orthodox science, Tiller proclaims the need for a new multidimensional model that takes into account the mind and intentionality, subtle energies, and the various unexplained psychic phenomena. He turns to superstring theory, with its tiny loops vibrating in multiple dimensions of hyperspace, and the simplicity that appears in the laws of nature from the multidimensional perspective that hyperspace offers. That is, when more dimensions are figured into the equations that describe physical phenomena, the equations simplify. They become elegant. Physicists and mathematicians perk up when that happens; they feel like they're on the right path to Truth. Tiller then proposes "The Tiller Model," starting from the premise that

> . . . We are primarily elements of spirit, indestruc-
> tible and eternal and "multiplexed" in the Divine. As
> such, we have a mechanism of perception which is a
> ten-dimensional mind domain. In turn, this mind
> mechanism creates a vehicle for our experience—our
> cosmos, our local universe, our solar system, our
> planet, our physical bodies, etc. This is all a "simu-
> lator" for our experience which we view from the spiri-
> tual level of self which is outside the simulator. Thus,
> we are spirits having a physical experience . . . The
> Simulator is a teaching machine of absolutely won-
> derful capabilities—created by God's love for us that
> we might experience and grow and be![13]

Tiller's mind mechanism is again resonant with Cayce's premise that "mind is the builder," and with the Cayce readings' founda-tional teaching that human existence is based in God's love and evolution toward union with the divine: "God, the Father, the first cause, seeking—in the manifestations of self—brought the world, as we (as individuals) observe it about us, into being—*through* love; giving to man, His creation, His creatures, that abil-ity to become one with Him." (262-46)

In more technical terms, Tiller's ten-dimensional model con-sists of what he calls "two interpenetrating and conjugate 4-spaces (the physical and the etheric substance domains that together form an 8 space) embedded in a 9 space (emotional domain) which is, in turn, embedded in a 10-space (mental do-main)."[14] This is a complicated way of saying that he sees the first four dimensions as the usual three dimensions of space and one of time, where electric matter has positive mass and travels at speeds slower than the speed of light (thus obeying Einstein's $E=mc^2$). This four-space is curved in such a way as to produce gravity; it's the world of physical matter. We're familiar with this world because we operate in it every day. It's the only world that the mechanistic view recognizes, despite the overwhelming evidence for more.

And part of the "more" as Tiller defines it is the next set of four dimensions. This set is reciprocal to the first set; they're a kind of "negative" of the first four, as photographs have negatives. This second 4-space, or set of four dimensions, is thus an inverse of the first set, and Tiller calls it a "frequency domain." Here is found magnetic matter of negative mass that actually travels faster than the speed of light, and the inherent curve produces levitational forces. This frequency domain is the ether, or the world of etheric matter. These two sets of four dimensions interlock with each other and mirror each other's properties (though not exactly by reflection), so that anything with a spatial pattern (that is, anything from the world of physical matter) has a counterpart that is a frequency pattern (that is, it also exists in the world of etheric matter). Tiller says it is the interactions between the two kinds of matter that gives rise to quantum mechanics: "It is precisely the direct space/inverse space pair of coordinate frames that lead to the wave/particle duality manifestations of nature on a microscopic level."[15] Tiller theorizes that a particle called the deltron mediates between the two realms and interacts with both physical particles that travel slower than the speed of light, and etheric particles that travel faster than the speed of light. In his model, it is this deltron that is sensitive to the focusing of human intention.

These eight dimensions are set in an emotional frame, which Tiller says can also be thought of as the astral level or plane. It is in this ninth level that deltrons originate. This is also the level of love, and mystics claim it is the level of relationship. These nine dimensions are embedded within a mind domain, which is a grid of nodal points. The tenth dimension of mind isn't a smooth continuum, but is granular and ordered. Tiller calls it "the primary lattice of nodal points" and says that it contains within itself "two sub-lattices which are both reciprocals of each other,"[16] that is, the two four-spaces, physical spacetime and the etheric domain, which are also grids. The physical domain is the coarsest grid, the etheric domain is the next-coarsest, and the mind domain is the finest grid. The three domains together form a network. Information waves, the essence of consciousness itself, travel along the nodal points of the network—which helps explain why remote viewing works, and why Cayce could accurately diagnose strangers from far away. Cayce, like the remote viewers psychically spying in the service of our country, picks up the information waves just as an antenna picks up radio waves. The future is accessible to the receivers, whether those viewers are Cayce or remote viewers or meditators, because future points are simply positions along the nodal network. And perhaps morphic fields, which carry accumulated memory and information, also travel along these nodes. In Tiller's model, the entire set of ten dimensions is held within the realm of spirit, the Divine level of self. Tiller proposes that "the boundary between the 10-dimensional domain of mind and the 11-dimensional domain of spirit is thought to distinguish and separate the *relative* universe (10-dimensional and below) from the *absolute* universe (11-dimensional and above)."[17]

Each domain is characterized by specific kinds of radiation. That is, in the material world, electromagnetic radiation is produced; in the etheric domain, magnetoelectric radiation, which travels faster than the speed of light, is present; and in the emotional or astral domain, deltrons are the radiation. While we can see, hear, feel, and otherwise access the effects of the physical plane, the etheric and astral domains are normally inaccessible to our senses. Unless, that is, we develop our senses; perception in the other realms consists of clairvoyance, clairaudience, etc. We do this by developing our coherence, which is the process of evolution. Tiller labels it in physics terms as a process of "negative entropy," that is, of increasing order. In fact, Tiller claims that developing our senses through increased coherence is one of the central tasks of human existence: "the whole purpose for the simulator is the human learning of applied intentionality and applied love in the evolution of self towards higher states of structural organization and consciousness."[18] Tiller is making the same point that the Cayce readings do, that we are here to love, to learn, and to evolve.

CHAPTER

7

I always wanted to write books. I read my first novel when I was six, a slim book called *Angel Unaware* that made an indelible impression on me. As an adult, I tracked down the book through the Internet and purchased it. When I was a kid, that book was so absorbing and wondrous to me that it inspired me to want to write. Nothing could be more exciting than to fire people's imaginations with words! Nothing could be more glamorous! Writing a book was a home run! And I kept encountering books that seized my soul in exactly the same fashion! So, when I was a little girl with long brown braids, knock knees, and too-big eyes, I jotted down poems and stories on lined paper, on the backs of envelopes, and on stiff napkins, and I pasted them inside brown pieces of cardboard, so they looked like books. This burning desire to write, and specifically to write books, has led me through my life. Literally. It took me into public libraries to read everything, rather indiscriminately, that I could lug out of the building. It prompted me to exclaim, "Yes!" when my high school boyfriend suggested that I go to college. It even steered me into a spiritual healing school, because I wanted to work through whatever blocks in my psyche and spirit were preventing me from actualizing myself as a writer, and because I wanted to be articulate with the language and literature of consciousness, to have access to those ideas in my writing.

I married during graduate school and had children shortly thereafter, and for fifteen years, I floundered in an abyss of writing poems, stories, non–fiction proposals, and novels that were vigorously rejected. At least I didn't give up; that's what having Terminator/Wonder Woman–like persistence will do for you: keep you persevering in the face of humiliating rejection, when a wiser, less stubborn individual would move on to something more rewarding. And there were some mitigating factors. For one, it's hard to simultaneously work and raise children as a deeply involved and conscientious mother. At least it's hard for me. Some women seem to accomplish it with ease. Maybe I'm just not organized enough or talented enough at multitasking, but for me, as a hands–on, down–in–the–trenches, leading–the–charge mom, everything came second to my children's needs. And two, I was developing my craft as a writer and earning my experience of the human condition. Time and space may be plastic and inconstant, but there's nothing like harsh miles and tough years to invest a mind and heart with artistic and intellectual authenticity. A rich life lived passionately, and thoughtfully, gives you something to say. Some gifted authors race right out of the starting box—and I would have enjoyed being one of them—but perhaps the most interesting, most flavorful stuff comes out of well–seasoned souls.

Part of my seasoning included the bitterness of divorce and the piquancy of new love, and something about the catastrophic changes in my life during those events pushed me to a new place in my career: I found myself with not one, but two contracts for books. I was given the opportunity to write this book, which involved research into topics which fascinate me, and a novel was picked up. The question is, what, apart from my life circumstances, changed, to allow this to happen?

The answer, of course, lies within my own consciousness. I changed internally. The way I thought about myself, my life, and my options changed. I restructured and refocused my mind, my beingness. Necessity was part of what drove this restructuring; I wasn't married to a businessman anymore, and that had serious financial consequences. There's nothing like a few bills to focus the mind. My intention shifted. So something about my inner world being focused and structured in a new way led to new results. Tiller comments on this process, explaining that, in terms of his model,

> **Intention imprints the desire of spirit onto the nodal network of mind. This mind-level information pattern imprints a correlate on the inverse space time domain and also activates the emotion frame to inject a higher density of deltrons into the interface between the relevant physical substance and its etheric counterpart. Thus, the etheric level information imprint is transferred from the magnetic frequency domain to the electric space-time domain and one detects materialization of the intention via our physical senses. It is important to recognize the importance of the individual's emotional strength here, because this is necessary for a strong final imprinting on the physical domain. Finally, it is important to recognize that action in the physical band of reality is the end result of a fairly significant sequence of steps initiated by spirit-directed intention. The unseen is the driver, the seen is the driven.[1]**

From this perspective, concrete results begin as desires in spirit, in the eleventh dimension. From there the pattern of the desire is, with intentionality, imprinted on the mind domain. Tiller says that "this pattern is an information pattern that is a one-to-one representation of the original intention."[2] Tiller further breaks down the level of mind into three substrata: instinctive mind, intellectual mind, and spiritual mind. The three levels of the mind domain, along with spirit, comprise the soul, and the etheric and physical levels of substance make up the body. Soul and body are connected by the emotional or astral level of substance, which Tiller calls the "'umbilical' cord that connects the Being to its containment vehicle."[3] He seems to agree with the seers who claim the astral domain is relational; the first relationship it modulates is the one between body and soul. So, in his model, desire originates in spirit and then is transferred to mind, and all this happens within the soul.

From the mind domain, the pattern is imprinted on the etheric substance of our being. Intentionality also galvanizes the emotional or astral frame, that ninth dimension where Tiller's deltrons originate and which links the soul with the body. It is this increased activity of the deltrons that does the imprinting from mind to etheric body, via a process described by the Fourier Transform, which boils down to: "The increased deltron activation strongly increases the coupling between the magnetic monopoles of R-space (the ether, or inverse spacetime) and the electric monopoles of D-space (the physical world, direct spacetime) so that the information pattern is transferred to D-space . . . These R-space/D-space information patterns engage the hard-wired mechanisms and processes of the physical body to materialize in physical reality the original intention."[4] That is, from the etheric domain, because of how strongly the deltrons yoke the etheric pattern to the physical domain, the desire becomes physical reality as we know it. It's a kind of condensation process, with the end product being a real event in physical spacetime. Tiller notes that the imprinting from spirit to mind is exact, but that the imprinting from mind to ether, and then from ether to physical reality, isn't quite perfect—which explains why the results can deviate, in greater or lesser degree, from the original desire.

Additionally, in Tiller's model, for this condensation or manifestation to occur, "spirit activates the driving consciousness wave pattern for its specific intention and the nodal points in the simulator convert these consciousness wave patterns into various kinds of energy wave patterns. These energy wave patterns communicate with the various types of particles and agglomerations of particles within the interstices of the appropriate nodal point network."[5] So consciousness waves make use of the nodes to propagate energy waves which, in turn, interact with particles like photons and bosons and gluons in the physical world, and with the correlates of those particles that exist in the etheric domain. Consciousness flows through the nodal network to generate deltrons and energy, which in turn generate substance. Strong energy waves mean strong interactions, and thus tightly hooked-up etheric and physical domains, and thus a stronger manifestation of desire into physical reality—more substance, sooner, that more closely reflects the original desire. The lattice-like or grid-like nodal networks, and the way they are mediated by deltrons from the emotion/astral domain, are, in this way, all important.

Earlier in this book, before discussions of horses and divorces, morphic fields and intentionality, quantum physics was discussed. Tiller's work takes its cue from the weirdness of quantum physics. He sets out from known quantum mechanical properties, such as the way a particle can dematerialize into the vacuum and rematerialize back out of the vacuum at another position in spacetime. He also makes use of the way "nature expresses itself simultaneously via its particle aspect and its wave aspect."[6] The physical domain expresses particles, and the ether, which is the inverse of the physical and is coupled with it, expresses waves. Since the velocity of a particle in our familiar space–time is less than the speed of light, and the velocity of a wave in the etheric domain is greater than the speed of light, relativity tells us that they could not interact. Since they clearly do, in Tiller's system, he ingeniously came up with something to couple them: deltrons, from the emotional domain. His solution resonates with the need for an observer, in quantum mechanics, to "collapse the wave" and trigger a quantum mechanical event. Consciousness factors in, in quantum physics—Tiller has theorized an explanation for how. He's pursued the implications of the effects of consciousness into the concrete arena of results in the real world. And in his model, the intensity of human intentionality influences the outcome of the event.

So, in my own life, the intensity of the restructuring of my life and my consciousness during and after my divorce allowed a process of manifestation to finally occur in my life. I manifested book contracts. But it wasn't just pure intensity which led to manifestation, although there was plenty of intensity during the divorce, as anyone who's been through one can confirm. The process was modulated by something else: increasing coherence. Tiller claims that "the structural character of the nodal networks are influenced by three main forces: (1) cosmological, (2) individual internal harmony versus disharmony and (3) collective humanity's internal harmony versus disharmony. When all the forces are beneficial, the nodal networks form relatively perfect lattices of very large extent and humans manifest fantastically large energy densities. When the reverse occurs, the nodal networks form an almost amorphous arrangement and humans manifest only very small amounts of life energy."[7] I would theorize that before my divorce, I had greater internal disharmony than after, and so I had less energy at my disposal to create the life I wanted. Despite the tears, battles, and legal fees, the experience led me to greater internal coherence and harmony. It seems that the yoga, prayer, meditation, and psychotherapy in which I engaged to support myself through the difficult life passage, and the hundred self-help books I read, did more than help me cope. Perhaps all of these aides thoroughly revamped my consciousness. The greater internal harmony that eventually blossomed allowed me to manifest my desires into my life in a way I hadn't been able to prior to then.

And it's not an accident that my life functioned this way. Tiller says, "The simulator is a device designed to teach us how to effectively use our intentionality. Since every application of our intention is an act of creation, it ultimately teaches us how to create properly, efficiently and effectively."[8] The "simulator" is my body-mind that travels through spacetime, my "entity-ness." The process of my life, of growing up as a Navy Brat, venturing off to college, marrying a man from a different religion whom I loved deeply but with whom I couldn't stay lovingly connected, slogging through the turmoil of divorce, gingerly setting up a new life for myself, taking the fearsome leap of faith into a new marriage—all this was the process of learning to use my intention. My life is my evolutionary lesson. Science and spirit both tell me so. As Cayce remarked, "Each may find within self the truth, the love, the life. Life is, in all its manifestations in every animate force, creative force in action; and is the love of expression—or expressing that life; truth becoming a result of life's love expressed. For, these are but names—unless experienced in the consciousness of each soul." (262-46) Moreover, evolution, memory, creativity, resonance, and consciousness, in forms like Sheldrake's morphic fields and Tiller's ten-dimensional model, flow through me. They aren't separate and apart from me. They inhabit me and I inhabit them, so that I can never separate myself from the dynamic field processes that animate the universe. Earlier in this book, I recounted how Cayce had the experience of traveling through water in a bubble to reach and retrieve the Akashic Records. But I understand the process of prophecy differently, because I have the benefit of learning about Sheldrake's morphic fields and Tiller's ten–dimensional mind domain. I understand that I don't have to travel to the Akashic Records. I'm living them. They permeate me. Magic and prophecy are threaded into my cells, and I myself am co–evolving with the universe.

Having come to understand that I am in a process of evolution which science as well as spirituality describes, I have come to agree with Tiller that

> **Our task is to transform the largely incoherent ingredients into a completely coherent system—and not just at the physical levels but at all the subtle levels as well. In our homes and schools we learn and practice many forms of athletics which discipline us to develop coordination, motor function skills and organized muscle systems as well as exercising our ability to focus intentionality on the "game." We begin to learn about relationships, about sharing, caring and appreciating and, as well, about loving. Thus, we develop levels of organization and order at the emotional domain level as well as at the physical domain level. This becomes further developed by our growing appreciation for music and art. Of course, our intellectual development as a component of our mind domain properties is not neglected and organized states of order develop here as well. Thus, we have already been moving down the path towards coherence without realizing it.[9]**

Tiller offers examples of methodologies like Qigong, yoga, and HeartMath techniques as "inner self–management practices." That is, they lead to greater internal coherence. This is simply another way of saying that we undertake transformation in order to personally experience the scientific and mystical act of piercing time and space. Regular meditation and prayer, a practice of yoga, and psychotherapy, and, for some people, attending religious services, also soften the jagged edges that we all have. So do working through the barriers to intimacy in personal relationships and practicing reverence, compassion, honesty, integrity, forgiveness, self-restraint, and so forth. Taped up on my refrigerator is a quote from Siddhartha Gautama: "The Buddha teaches this triple truth to all: a generous heart, kind speech, and a life of service and compassion are the things which renew humanity." But all the great religions say something similar at their core. These aforementioned pursuits are only some of the myriad paths to inner coherence, of course. A friend of mine says that fishing is prayer and worship for him. I've been out with him on his little motor boat in the Pamet Bay of Cape Cod, and while I've never understood why he believes that bluefish chomping on a school of bait fish releases a scent like cucumbers, I do grasp his point about fishing as transformation. Being out on the water under a glorious bright sun and limitless blue sky nurtures the soul. Something smooth and expansive opens up, in the mind, in the heart, and in the spirit. That expansive flowing thing is grace, a connection to the Divine. I've had the same experience on the back of a horse on a trail in the woods, on a spring morning with new life welling up everywhere around me: in purply-green tree buds, shrill bird calls, and a warming breeze. I've felt it in my children's arms as well as in meditation retreats. I've even seen it in the eyes of my ex-husband during the most painful moments of our hostilities, because I showed up for the experience, and simply being present in the moment is itself a crucible that can lead me into the process of evolution. And I've read about it in Edgar Cayce's transcripts, in Sheldrake's work on the theory of formative causation, and in Tiller's physics-based books on human consciousness. These are all paths to evolution; what's important isn't the specifics of those paths, but that they are taken. When they are, we come into our birthright as children of the Divine. We're granted opportunities to create our lives, to write the books of our lives, as we want them to be. We get to compose our own Akashic Records. For me, that meant physically writing books.

So one of the paths to evolution—to grace and authorial license and union with the divine—is science. Science has been seen by modernity as a codification of the rules by which the machine-like universe works, as the very antithesis of soul and the miraculous, but that view is changing. In the new paradigm, science is softening, opening up, taking on the slippery attributes of mysticism. Science has begun to embrace magic. Sheldrake says, "Like the world of the magician, the world of the physicist is full of unseen connections traversing apparently empty space."[10] Sheldrake makes an argument for how morphic fields transcend time and space to shape form and evolution, from the biological to the cultural, from the individual to the species; Tiller shows how human intentionality breaches time and space to create reality. Part of the purpose of this book is to empower people in their intentionality toward their own lives. In the twenty-first century, because we are surrounded by the fruits of science, from the Internet to television to medicine, we are all influenced by science. To see in detail how science parallels and supports the mystical aspects of life is to persuade ourselves that mysticism is real and that consciousness matters. We become convinced of the truth of what Cayce often said: "Mind is the builder." It's intrinsic to human nature to want to build something better, so we grow more aware of, and more responsible for, ourselves, our thoughts, our biases, and our assumptions. We have an opportunity to grow in tolerance and understanding, and by so doing, to heal ourselves, humanity, and the world. When time and space fall away, so do polarities. We ourselves become like Tiller's deltrons, coupling the physical world to the immanent and transcendent metaphysical world: living embodiments of union.

Notes

Introduction

1. Rupert Sheldrake, *A New Science of Life: The Hypothesis of Morphic Resonance* (Rochester, VT: Park Street Press, 1981) p. 13.
2. Rupert Sheldrake, *The Presence of the Past: Morphic Resonance & The Habits of Nature* (Rochester, VT: Park Street Press, 1988) p. xvii.
3. Rupert Sheldrake, *Seven Experiments that Could Change the World* (Rochester, Vermont: Park Street Press, 1995) p. 244.
4. Sheldrake, *Seven Experiments that Could Change the World*, p. 106.
5. William Tiller, *Science and Human Transformation: Subtle Energies, Intentionality and Consciousness* (Walnut Creek, CA: Pavior Books, 1997) p. 55.

Chapter 1

1. Jess Stearn, *Edgar Cayce: The Sleeping Prophet* (New York: Bantam Books, 1968) p. 13.
2. Stanley Kirkpatrick, *Edgar Cayce: An American Prophet* (New York: Riverhead Books, 2000) p. 21.
3. Kirkpatrick, p. 37.
4. Stearn, p. 28.
5. Kirkpatrick, p. 96.

6. Kirkpatrick, p. 98.
7. Kirkpatrick, p. 110.
8. Kirkpatrick, p. 116.
9. Kirkpatrick, pp. 117–118.
10. Kirkpatrick, p. 144.

Chapter 2

1. Moray B. King, *Tapping the Zero-Point Energy* (Provo, UT: Paraclete Publishing, 1989) p. 2.
2. King, p. 3.

3. Margaret Cheney, *Tesla: Man Out of Time* (New York: Barnes and Nobles Books, 1983) p. 2.
4. Cheney, p. 271.
5. Fritjof Capra, *The Web of Life* (New York: Doubleday Books, 1996) p. 30.
6. Brian Greene, *The Elegant Universe: Superstrings, Hidden Dimensions, and the Quest for the Ultimate Theory* (New York: Norton & Co., 1999) p. 129.
7. Rupert Sheldrake, *The Presence of the Past: Morphic Resonance and the Habits of Nature* (Rochester, VT: Park Street Press, 1995) p. 304.
8. Swami Harshananda, *Hindu Gods and Goddesses* (Mylapore, Chennai: Sri Ramakrishna Math) p. xi.
9. Gladys Davis' note in Reading 245-1 (6).
10. Komilla Sutton, *The Lunar Nodes: Crisis and Redemption* (Bournemouth, England: The Wessex Astrologer Ltd, 2001) pp. 10—11.
11. Greene, p. 15.
12. Greene, p. 146.
13. William Tiller, *Science and Human Transformation: Subtle Energies, Intentionality, and Consciousness* (Walnut Creek, CA: Pavior Publishing, 1997) p. 49.
14. Michio Kaku, *Hyperspace: A Scientific Odyssey Through Parallel Universes, Time Warps, and the Tenth Dimension* (New York: Doubleday Books, 1994) pp. 153-154.

Chapter 3
1. Moray B. King, *Tapping the Zero Point Energy* (Provo, UT: Paraclete Publishing, 1989) p. 107.
2. Fritjof Capra, *The Web of Life* (New York: Doubleday Books, 1996) p. 6.
3. Capra, p. 6.
4. Cecilia Goodnow, "Think someone's staring at you? 'Sixth Sense' may be biological," *Seattle Post Intelligencer* 1 April 2003,

reprinted by permission on Rupert Sheldrake's Web site, www.sheldrake.org/books_tapes/staring_interview_SeattlePI.html.

5. King, p. 114.
6. Rupert Sheldrake, *A New Science of Life: The Hypothesis of Morphic Resonance* (Rochester, VT: Park Street Press, 1981) p. 13.
7. Sheldrake, *A New Science of Life*, p. 19.
8. Robert Becker, *The Body Electric: Electromagnetism and the Foundation of Life* (New York: William Morrow, 1985) pp. 155–157.
9. Sheldrake, *A New Science of Life*, p. 28.
10. Sheldrake, *A New Science of Life* p. 27.
11. Sheldrake, *A New Science of Life* p. 48.
12. Sheldrake, *A New Science of Life* p. 71.
13. Sheldrake, *A New Science of Life* p. 72.
14. Sheldrake, *A New Science of Life* p. 93.
15. Sheldrake, *A New Science of Life* p. 95.
16 Rupert Sheldrake, *Seven Experiments that Could Change the World: A Do-it-Yourself Guide to Revolutionary Science* (Rochester, VT: Park Street Press, 2002) pp. xiii–xv
17. Rupert Sheldrake, *The Presence of the Past: Morphic Resonance & the Habits of Nature* (Rochester, VT: Park Street Press, 1988) p. 25.
18. Sheldrake, *The Presence of the Past*, p. 29.
19. Sheldrake, *The Presence of the Past*, p. 70.

Chapter 4

1. Rupert Sheldrake, *The Presence of the Past: Morphic Resonance and the Habits of Nature* (Rochester, VT: Park Street Press, 1995), pp. 88–90.
2. Sheldrake, *The Presence of the Past*, p. 136.
3. Ibid.
4. Sheldrake, *The Presence of the Past*, p. 108.
5. Sheldrake, *The Presence of the Past*, p. 109.

6. Sheldrake, *The Presence of the Past,* p. 303.
7. Ibid.
8. Sheldrake, *The Presence of the Past,* p. 120.
9. Sheldrake, *The Presence of the Past,* p. 146.
10. Sheldrake, *The Presence of the Past,* pp. 157–158.
11. Sheldrake, *The Presence of the Past,* pp. 174.
12. Ibid.
13. Sheldrake, *The Presence of the Past,* p. 175.
14. Sheldrake, *The Presence of the Past,* p. 181.
15. Sheldrake, *The Presence of the Past,* p. 190.
16. Rupert Sheldrake, Terrence McKenna, and Ralph Abraham, *Chaos, Creativity, and Cosmic Consciousness* (Rochester, VT: Park Street Press, 2001) p. 27.

Chapter 5
1. Rupert Sheldrake, *Seven Experiments that Could Change the World: A Do-It-Yourself Guide to Revolutionary Science* (Rochester, VT: Park Street Press, 2002) p. 144.
2. William Tiller, *Science and Human Transformation: Subtle Energies, Intentionality, and Consciousness* (Walnut Creek, CA: Pavior Publishing, 1997) p. 152.

Chapter 6
1. Vladimir Nabokov, *Lolita* (New York, NY: Perigee Books, 1980) p. 311.
2. William Tiller, *Conscious Acts of Creation: The Emergence of a New Physics* (Walnut Creek, CA: Pavior Publishing, 2001) p. 1.
3. William Tiller, *Science and Human Transformation: Subtle Energies, Intentionality, and Consciousness* (Walnut Creek, CA: Pavior Publishing, 1997) p. 179.
4. Tiller, *Science and Human Transformation,* p. 2.
5. Ibid.
6. Tiller, *Science and Human Transformation,* p.3.

7. Tiller, *Science and Human Transformation*, p. 4.
8. Rupert Sheldrake, *The Presence of the Past: Morphic Resonance and the Habits of Nature* (Rochester, VT: Park Street Press, 1995) p. 304.
9. Tiller, *Science and Human Transformation*, p. 12.
10. Tiller, *Science and Human Transformation*, pp. 20–21.
11. See Joseph McMoneagle, *Remote Viewing Secrets: A Handbook* (Charlottesville, VA: Hampton Roads Publishing Co., 2000), Joseph McMoneagle, *Mind Trek: Exploring Consciousness, Time and Space through Remote Viewing* (Charlottesville, VA: Hampton Roads Publishing Co., 1997), and David Morehouse, *Psychic Warrior* (New York, NY: St. Martin's Press, 1997).
12. Tiller, *Science and Human Transformation*, p. 23.
13. Tiller, *Science and Human Transformation*, p. 55.
14. Ibid.
15. Tiller, *Science and Human Transformation*, p. 56.
16. Tiller, *Science and Human Transformation*, p. 58.
17. Tiller, *Conscious Acts of Creation*, p. 26.
18. Tiller, *Science and Human Transformation*, p. 67.

Chapter 7
1. William Tiller, *Science and Human Transformation: Subtle Energies, Intentionality, and Consciousness* (Walnut Creek, CA: Pavior Publishing, 1997) p. 84.
2. William Tiller, *Conscious Acts of Creation: The Emergence of a New Physics* (Walnut Creek, CA: Pavior Publishing, 2001) p. 27.
3. Tiller, *Science and Human Transformation*, p. 87.
4. Ibid.
5. Tiller, *Conscious Acts of Creation*, p. 311.
6. Tiller, *Conscious Acts of Creation*, p. 23.
7. Tiller, *Science and Human Transformation*, p. 89.
8. Ibid.
9. Tiller, *Science and Human Transformation*, p. 198.

10. Rupert Sheldrake, *The Presence of the Past: Morphic Resonance and the Habits of Nature* (Rochester, VT: Park Street Press, 1995), p. 315.

Bibliography

Becker, Robert. *The Body Electric: Electromagnetism and the Foundation of Life.* New York: William Morrow, 1985.

Bohm, David. *Wholeness and the Implicate Order.* London: Ark Paperbacks, 1983.

Capra, Fritjof. *The Web of Life: A New Scientific Understanding of Living Systems.* New York: Doubleday Books, 1996.

Cayce, Hugh Lynn, ed. *The Edgar Cayce Reader: Volume 1.* New York: Warner Books, 1988.

—. *The Edgar Cayce Reader: Volume 2.* New York: Warner Books, 1988.

Cheney, Margaret. *Tesla: Man Out of Time.* New York: Barnes and Nobles Books, 1983.

Friedman, Norman. *The Hidden Domain: Home of the Quantum Wave Function, Nature's Creative Source.* Eugene, OR: The Woodbridge Group, 1997.

Goodnow, Cecilia. "Think someone's staring at you? 'Sixth Sense' may be biological," *Seattle Post Intelligencer* 1 April 2003, reprinted by permission on Rupert Sheldrake's web site, www.sheldrake.org.

Gott, J. Richard, *Time Travel in Einstein's Universe: The Physical Possibilities of Travel Through Time.* New York: Mariner Books, 2002.

Greene, Brian. *The Elegant Universe: Superstrings, Hidden Dimensions, and the Quest for the Ultimate Theory.* New York: Norton & Co., 1999.

Kaku, Michio. *Hyperspace: A Scientific Odyssey Through Parallel Universes, Time Warps, and the Tenth Dimension*. New York: Doubleday Books, 1994.

King, Moray B. *Tapping the Zero-Point Energy*. Provo, UT: Paraclete Publishing, 1989.

Kirkpatrick, Stanley. *Edgar Cayce: An American Prophet*. New York: Riverhead Books, 2000.

Mlodinow, Leonard. *Feynman's Rainbow: A Search for Beauty in Physics and in Life*. New York: Warner Books, 2003.

Nabokov, Vladimir. *Lolita*. New York, NY: Perigee Books, 1980.

Puryear, Herbert B. *The Edgar Cayce Primer: Discovering the Path to Self-Transformation*. New York: Bantam Books, 1982.

Sheldrake, Rupert. *A New Science of Life: Morphic Resonance and the Habits of Nature*. Rochester, VT: Park Street Press, 1995.

—. *The Presence of the Past: Morphic Resonance and the Habits of Nature*. Rochester, VT: Park Street Press, 1995.

—. *Seven Experiments that Could Change the World: A Do-It-Yourself Guide to Revolutionary Science*. Rochester, VT: Park Street Press, 2002.

Sheldrake, Rupert, Terrence McKenna, and Ralph Abraham, *Chaos, Creativity, and Cosmic Consciousness*. Rochester, VT: Park Street Press, 2001.

Stearn, Jess. *Edgar Cayce: The Sleeping Prophet*. New York: Bantam Books, 1968.

Sutton, Komilla. *The Lunar Nodes: Crisis and Redemption*. Bournemouth, England: The Wessex Astrologer Ltd, 2001.

Swami Harshananda, *Hindu Gods and Goddesses*. Mylapore, Chennai: Sri Ramakrishna Math.

Thurston, Mark and Christopher Fazel. *The Edgar Cayce Handbook for Creating Your Future*. New York: Ballantine Books, 1992.

Tiller, William. *Conscious Acts of Creation: The Emergence of a New Physics*.Walnut Creek, CA: Pavior Publishing, 2001.

—. *Science and Human Transformation: Subtle Energies, Intentionality, and Consciousness*. Walnut Creek, CA: Pavior Publishing, 1997.

A.R.E. PRESS

The A.R.E. Press publishes books, videos, and audiotapes meant to improve the quality of our readers' lives—personally, professionally, and spiritually. We hope our products support your endeavors to realize your career potential, to enhance your relationships, to improve your health, and to encourage you to make the changes necessary to live a loving, joyful, and fulfilling life.

For more information or to receive a free catalog, call:

1–800–723–1112

Or write:

A.R.E. Press
215 67th Street
Virginia Beach, VA 23451–2061

DISCOVER HOW THE EDGAR CAYCE MATERIAL CAN HELP YOU!

The Association for Research and Enlightenment, Inc. (A.R.E.®), was founded in 1931 by Edgar Cayce. Its international headquarters are in Virginia Beach, Virginia, where thousands of visitors come year–round. Many more are helped and inspired by A.R.E.'s local activities in their own hometowns or by contact via mail (and now the Internet!) with A.R.E. headquarters.

People from all walks of life, all around the world, have discovered meaningful and life–transforming insights in the A.R.E. programs and materials, which focus on such areas as personal spirituality, holistic health, dreams, family life, finding your best vocation, reincarnation, ESP, meditation, and soul growth in small–group settings. Call us today at our toll–free number:

1–800–333–4499

or

Explore our electronic visitors center on the
Internet: **http://www.edgarcayce.org.**

We'll be happy to tell you more about how the work of the A.R.E. can help you!

A.R.E.
215 67th Street
Virginia Beach, VA 23451–2061